Constitutional Law

Third Edition

2010 Supplement

ASPEN PUBLISHERS

2010 Supplement

Constitutional Law

Third Edition

Erwin Chemerinsky
Dean and Distinguished Professor of Law
University of California, Irvine, School of Law

Wolters Kluwer
Law & Business

AUSTIN   BOSTON   CHICAGO   NEW YORK   THE NETHERLANDS

To contact Customer Care, e-mail customer.service@aspenpublishers.com, call 1-800-234-1660, fax 1-800-901-9075, or mail correspondence to:

>Aspen Publishers
>Attn: Order Department
>PO Box 990
>Frederick, MD 21705

Printed in the United States of America.

1 2 3 4 5 6 7 8 9 0

ISBN 978-0-7355-9036-6

Library of Congress Cataloging-in-Publication Data

Chemerinsky, Erwin.
 Constitutional law/Erwin Chemerinsky.—3rd ed.
  p. cm.
 Includes bibliographical references and index.
 ISBN 978-0-7355-7717-6 (casebook)
 ISBN 978-0-7355-9036-6 (supplement)
 1. Constitutional law—United States—Cases. I. Title.

 KF4549.C44 2009
 342.73—dc22

                                               2009008261

About Wolters Kluwer Law & Business

Wolters Kluwer Law & Business is a leading provider of research information and workflow solutions in key specialty areas. The strengths of the individual brands of Aspen Publishers, CCH, Kluwer Law International and Loislaw are aligned within Wolters Kluwer Law & Business to provide comprehensive, in-depth solutions and expert-authored content for the legal, professional and education markets.

CCH was founded in 1913 and has served more than four generations of business professionals and their clients. The CCH products in the Wolters Kluwer Law & Business group are highly regarded electronic and print resources for legal, securities, antitrust and trade regulation, government contracting, banking, pension, payroll, employment and labor, and healthcare reimbursement and compliance professionals.

Aspen Publishers is a leading information provider for attorneys, business professionals and law students. Written by preeminent authorities, Aspen products offer analytical and practical information in a range of specialty practice areas from securities law and intellectual property to mergers and acquisitions and pension/benefits. Aspen's trusted legal education resources provide professors and students with high-quality, up-to-date and effective resources for successful instruction and study in all areas of the law.

Kluwer Law International supplies the global business community with comprehensive English-language international legal information. Legal practitioners, corporate counsel and business executives around the world rely on the Kluwer Law International journals, loose-leafs, books and electronic products for authoritative information in many areas of international legal practice.

Loislaw is a premier provider of digitized legal content to small law firm practitioners of various specializations. Loislaw provides attorneys with the ability to quickly and efficiently find the necessary legal information they need, when and where they need it, by facilitating access to primary law as well as state-specific law, records, forms and treatises.

Wolters Kluwer Law & Business, a unit of Wolters Kluwer, is headquartered in New York and Riverwoods, Illinois. Wolters Kluwer is a leading multinational publisher and information services company.

Contents

Preface

The third edition of *Constitutional Law* was published in the spring of 2009 and is complete through the end of October Term 2007, which ended on June 26, 2008. This supplement covers the major decisions of October Term 2008, which ended on June 29, 2009, and October Term 2009, which ended on June 28, 2010.

As with past supplements, the new cases are presented in the context of the section of the casebook where they would fit. Brief introductory notes provide students information on how the new cases relate to the prior decisions.

I will prepare annual supplements and look forward to the Fourth Edition in 2013. Suggestions from professors and students are invaluable and very much appreciated.

Erwin Chemerinsky
July 2010

Chapter 1

The Federal Judicial Power

B. Limits on the Federal Judicial Power

1. Interpretive limits

How should the Second Amendment be interpreted? Consider the Second Amendment as an example (casebook, p. 13).

In *District of Columbia v. Heller* (casebook, p. 13), the Supreme Court held that the Second Amendment protects a right of individuals to have guns, at least in their homes, for self-protection. In *McDonald v. City of Chicago* (2010), the Court held that this right applies to state and local governments. *McDonald* is presented in Chapter 5 below in connection with the material on the application of the Bill of Rights to the states.

Chapter 2

The Federal Legislative Power

A. Introduction: Congress and the States (casebook, p. 127)

In *McCulloch v. Maryland* (p. 129), the Court discusses the "necessary and proper clause" found in Article I of the Constitution. In *United States v. Comstock* (2010), the Court engaged in detailed analysis and use of the necessary and proper clause. The Court expressly invoked and relied on *McCulloch*.

U.S. v. COMSTOCK
130 S.Ct. 1949 (2010)

Justice BREYER delivered the opinion of the Court.

A federal civil-commitment statute authorizes the Department of Justice to detain a mentally ill, sexually dangerous federal prisoner beyond the date the prisoner would otherwise be released. We have previously examined similar statutes enacted under state law to determine whether they violate the Due Process Clause. See *Kansas v. Hendricks,* (1997); *Kansas v. Crane* (2002). But this case presents a different question. Here we ask whether the Federal Government has the authority under Article I of the Constitution to enact this federal civil-commitment program or whether its doing so falls beyond the reach of a government "of enumerated powers." *McCulloch v. Maryland* (1819). We conclude that the Constitution grants Congress the authority to enact § 4248 as "necessary and proper for carrying into Execution" the powers "vested by" the "Constitution in the Government of the United States.

I

The federal statute before us allows a district court to order the civil commitment of an individual who is currently "in the custody of the [Federal] Bureau of Prisons," if that individual (1) has previously "engaged or attempted to engage in sexually violent conduct or child molestation," (2) currently "suffers from a serious mental illness, abnormality, or disorder," and (3) "as a result of" that mental illness, abnormality, or disorder is "sexually dangerous to others," in that "he would have serious difficulty in refraining from sexually violent conduct or child molestation if released."

In order to detain such a person, the Government (acting through the Department of Justice) must certify to a federal district judge that the prisoner meets the conditions just described, *i.e.,* that he has engaged in sexually violent activity or child molestation in the past and that he suffers from a mental illness that makes him correspondingly dangerous to others. When such a certification is filed, the statute automatically stays the individual's release from prison, thereby giving the Government an opportunity to prove its claims at a hearing through psychiatric (or other) evidence. The statute provides that the prisoner "shall be represented by counsel" and shall have "an opportunity" at the hearing "to testify, to present evidence, to subpoena witnesses on his behalf, and to confront and cross-examine" the Government's witnesses.

If the Government proves its claims by "clear and convincing evidence," the court will order the prisoner's continued commitment in "the custody of the Attorney General," who must "make all reasonable efforts to cause" the State where that person was tried, or the State where he is domiciled, to "assume responsibility for his custody, care, and treatment." If either State is willing to assume that responsibility, the Attorney General "shall release" the individual "to the appropriate official" of that State. But if, "notwithstanding such efforts, neither such State will assume such responsibility," then "the Attorney General shall place the person for treatment in a suitable [federal] facility."

Confinement in the federal facility will last until either (1) the person's mental condition improves to the point where he is no longer dangerous (with or without appropriate ongoing treatment), in which case he will be released; or (2) a State assumes responsibility for his custody, care, and treatment, in which case he will be transferred to the custody of that State. The statute establishes a system for ongoing psychiatric and judicial review of the individual's case, including judicial hearings at the request of the confined person at six-month intervals.

In November and December 2006, the Government instituted proceedings in the Federal District Court for the Eastern District of North Carolina against the five respondents in this case. Three of the five had previously pleaded guilty in federal court to possession of child pornography, and the fourth had pleaded guilty to sexual abuse of a minor.

With respect to each of them, the Government claimed that the respondent was about to be released from federal prison, that he had engaged in sexually violent conduct or child molestation in the past, and that he suffered from a mental illness that made him sexually dangerous to others. During that same time period, the Government instituted similar proceedings against the fifth respondent, who had been charged in federal court with aggravated sexual abuse of a minor, but was found mentally incompetent to stand trial. Each of the five respondents moved to dismiss the civil-commitment proceeding on constitutional grounds.

II

The question presented is whether the Necessary and Proper Clause, Art. I, § 8, cl. 18, grants Congress authority sufficient to enact the statute before us. In resolving that question, we assume, but we do not decide, that other provisions of the Constitution-such as the Due Process Clause-do not prohibit civil commitment in these circumstances. In other words, we assume for argument's sake that the Federal Constitution would permit a State to enact this statute, and we ask solely whether the Federal Government, exercising its enumerated powers, may enact such a statute as well. On that assumption, we conclude that the Constitution grants Congress legislative power sufficient to enact § 4248. We base this conclusion on five considerations, taken together.

First, the Necessary and Proper Clause grants Congress broad authority to enact federal legislation. Nearly 200 years ago, this Court stated that the Federal "[G]overnment is acknowledged by all to be one of enumerated powers," *McCulloch,* which means that "[e]very law enacted by Congress must be based on one or more of" those powers. But, at the same time, "a government, entrusted with such" powers "must also be entrusted with ample means for their execution." Accordingly, the Necessary and Proper Clause makes clear that the Constitution's grants of specific federal legislative authority are accompanied by broad power to enact laws that are "convenient, or useful" or "conducive" to the authority's "beneficial exercise." "Let the end be legitimate, let it be within the scope of the constitution, and all means which are appropriate, which are plainly adapted to that end, which are not prohibited, but consist with the letter and spirit of the constitution, are constitutional."

We have since made clear that, in determining whether the Necessary and Proper Clause grants Congress the legislative authority to enact a particular federal statute, we look to see whether the statute constitutes a means that is rationally related to the implementation of a constitutionally enumerated power.

We have also recognized that the Constitution "addresse[s]" the "choice of means" "primarily . . . to the judgment of Congress. If it can be seen that the means adopted are really calculated to attain the end, the degree of their necessity, the extent to which they conduce to the end, the closeness of the relationship between the means adopted and the end to be attained, are matters for congressional determination alone."

Thus, the Constitution, which nowhere speaks explicitly about the creation of federal crimes beyond those related to "counterfeiting," "treason," or "Piracies and Felonies committed on the high Seas" or "against the Law of Nations," nonetheless grants Congress broad authority to create such crimes. And Congress routinely exercises its authority to enact criminal laws in furtherance of, for example, its enumerated powers to regulate interstate and foreign commerce, to enforce civil rights, to spend funds for the general welfare, to establish federal courts, to establish post offices, to regulate bankruptcy, to regulate naturalization, and so forth.

Similarly, Congress, in order to help ensure the enforcement of federal criminal laws enacted in furtherance of its enumerated powers, "can cause a prison to be erected at any place within the jurisdiction of the United States, and direct that all persons sentenced to imprisonment under the laws of the United States shall be confined there." Moreover, Congress, having established a prison system, can enact laws that seek to ensure that system's safe and responsible administration by, for example, requiring prisoners to receive medical care and educational training, and can also ensure the safety of the prisoners, prison workers and visitors, and those in surrounding communities by, for example, creating further criminal laws governing entry, exit, and smuggling, and by employing prison guards to ensure discipline and security.

Neither Congress' power to criminalize conduct, nor its power to imprison individuals who engage in that conduct, nor its power to enact laws governing prisons and prisoners, is explicitly mentioned in the Constitution. But Congress nonetheless possesses broad authority to do each of those things in the course of "carrying into Execution" the enumerated powers "vested by" the "Constitution in the Government of the United States."

Second, the civil-commitment statute before us constitutes a modest addition to a set of federal prison-related mental-health statutes that have existed for many decades. We recognize that even a longstanding history of related federal action does not demonstrate a statute's constitutionality.

A history of involvement, however, can nonetheless be "helpful in reviewing the substance of a congressional statutory scheme," and, in particular, the reasonableness of the relation between the new statute and pre-existing federal interests.

Here, Congress has long been involved in the delivery of mental health care to federal prisoners, and has long provided for their civil commitment. In 1855 it established Saint Elizabeth's Hospital in the District of Columbia to provide treatment to "the insane of the army and navy . . . and of the District of Columbia." In 1857 it provided for confinement at Saint Elizabeth's of any person within the District of Columbia who had been "charged with [a] crime" and who was "insane" or later became "insane during the continuance of his or her sentence in the United States penitentiary." In 1874, expanding the geographic scope of its statutes, Congress provided for civil commitment in federal facilities (or in state facilities if a State so agreed) of *"all* persons who have been or shall be convicted of any offense in *any* court of the United States" and who are or "shall become" insane "during the term of their imprisonment." And in 1882 Congress provided for similar commitment of those *"charged"* with federal offenses who become "insane" while in the "custody" of the United States. Thus, over the span of three decades, Congress created a national, federal civil-commitment program under which any person who was either charged with or convicted of any federal offense in any federal court could be confined in a federal mental institution.

In 2006, Congress enacted the particular statute before us. 18 U.S.C. § 4248. It differs from earlier statutes in that it focuses directly upon persons who, due to a mental illness, are sexually dangerous. Notably, many of these individuals were likely already subject to civil commitment under § 4246, which, since 1949, has authorized the postsentence detention of federal prisoners who suffer from a mental illness and who are thereby dangerous (whether sexually or otherwise). Aside from its specific focus on sexually dangerous persons, § 4248 is similar to the provisions first enacted in 1949. In that respect, it is a modest addition to a longstanding federal statutory framework, which has been in place since 1855.

Third, Congress reasonably extended its longstanding civil-commitment system to cover mentally ill and sexually dangerous persons who are already in federal custody, even if doing so detains them beyond the termination of their criminal sentence. For one thing, the Federal Government is the custodian of its prisoners. As federal custodian, it has the constitutional power to act in order to protect nearby (and other) communities from the danger federal prisoners may pose. If a federal prisoner is infected with a communicable disease that threatens others, surely it would be "necessary and proper" for the Federal Government to take action, pursuant to its role as federal custodian, to refuse (at least until the threat diminishes) to release that individual among the general public, where he might infect others. And if confinement of such an individual is a "necessary and proper" thing to do, then how could it not be similarly "necessary and proper" to confine an individual whose mental illness threatens others to the same degree?

Moreover, § 4248 is "reasonably adapted," to Congress' power to act as a responsible federal custodian. Congress could have reasonably concluded that federal inmates who suffer from a mental illness that causes them to "have serious difficulty in refraining from sexually violent conduct," would pose an especially high danger to the public if released. And Congress could also have reasonably concluded (as detailed in the Judicial Conference's report) that a reasonable number of such individuals would likely *not* be detained by the States if released from federal custody, in part because the Federal Government itself severed their claim to "legal residence in any State" by incarcerating them in remote federal prisons.

Fourth, the statute properly accounts for state interests. Respondents and the dissent contend that § 4248 violates the Tenth Amendment because it "invades the province of state sovereignty" in an area typically left to state control. But the Tenth Amendment's text is clear: "The powers *not delegated to the United States* by the Constitution, nor prohibited by it to the States, are reserved to the States respectively, or to the people." The powers "delegated to the United States by the Constitution" include those specifically enumerated powers listed in Article I along with the implementation authority granted by the Necessary and Proper Clause. Virtually by definition, these powers are not powers that the Constitution "reserved to the States."

Nor does this statute invade state sovereignty or otherwise improperly limit the scope of "powers that remain with the States." To the contrary, it requires *accommodation* of state interests.

Fifth, the links between § 4248 and an enumerated Article I power are not too attenuated. Neither is the statutory provision too sweeping in its scope. Invoking the cautionary instruction that we may not "pile inference upon inference" in order to sustain congressional action under Article I, respondents argue that, when legislating pursuant to the Necessary and Proper Clause, Congress' authority can be no more than one step removed from a specifically enumerated power. But this argument is irreconcilable with our precedents. And, as we have explained, from the implied power to punish we have *further* inferred both the power to imprison, and, in *Greenwood,* the federal civil-commitment power.

Indeed even the dissent acknowledges that Congress has the implied power to criminalize any conduct that might interfere with the exercise of an enumerated power, and also the additional power to imprison people who violate those (inferentially authorized) laws, and the additional power to provide for the safe and reasonable management of those prisons, and the additional power to regulate the prisoners' behavior even after their release. And the same enumerated power that justifies the creation of a federal criminal statute, and that justifies the additional implied federal powers that the dissent considers legitimate, justifies civil commitment under § 4248 as well. Thus, we must reject respondents' argument that the Necessary and Proper Clause permits no more than a single step between an enumerated power and an Act of Congress.

Nor need we fear that our holding today confers on Congress a general "police power, which the Founders denied the National Government and reposed in the States." As the Solicitor General repeatedly confirmed at oral argument, § 4248 is narrow in scope. It has been applied to only a small fraction of federal prisoners. Thus, far from a "general police power," § 4248 is a reasonably adapted and narrowly tailored means of pursuing the Government's legitimate interest as a federal custodian in the responsible administration of its prison system.

* * *

We take these five considerations together. They include: (1) the breadth of the Necessary and Proper Clause, (2) the long history of federal involvement in this arena, (3) the sound reasons for the statute's enactment in light of the Government's custodial interest in safeguarding the public from dangers posed by those in federal custody, (4) the statute's accommodation of state interests, and (5) the statute's narrow scope. Taken together, these considerations lead us to conclude that the statute is a "necessary and proper" means of exercising the federal authority that permits Congress to create federal criminal laws, to punish their violation, to imprison violators, to provide appropriately for those imprisoned, and to maintain the security of those who are not imprisoned but who may be affected by the federal imprisonment of others. The Constitution consequently authorizes Congress to enact the statute.

We do not reach or decide any claim that the statute or its application denies equal protection of the laws, procedural or substantive due process, or any other rights guaranteed by the Constitution. Respondents are free to pursue those claims on remand, and any others they have preserved.

Justice THOMAS, with whom Justice SCALIA joins.

The Court holds today that Congress has power under the Necessary and Proper Clause to enact a law authorizing the Federal Government to civilly commit "sexually dangerous person[s]" beyond the date it lawfully could hold them on a charge or conviction for a federal crime. I disagree. The Necessary and Proper Clause empowers Congress to enact only those laws that "carr[y] into Execution" one or more of the federal powers enumerated in the Constitution. Because § 4248 "Execut[es]" no enumerated power, I must respectfully dissent.

[I]

No enumerated power in Article I, § 8, expressly delegates to Congress the power to enact a civil-commitment regime for sexually dangerous persons, nor does any other provision in the Constitution vest Congress or the other branches of the Federal Government with such a power. Accordingly, § 4248 can be a valid exercise of congressional authority only if it is "necessary and proper for carrying into Execution" one or more of those federal powers actually enumerated in the Constitution.

Section 4248 does not fall within any of those powers. The Government identifies no specific enumerated power or powers as a constitutional predicate for § 4248, and none are readily discernable. Indeed, not even the Commerce Clause—the enumerated power this Court has interpreted most expansively, can justify federal civil detention of sex offenders. Under the Court's precedents, Congress may not regulate noneconomic activity (such as sexual violence) based solely on the effect such activity may have, in individual cases or in the aggregate, on interstate commerce. That limitation forecloses any claim that § 4248 carries into execution Congress' Commerce Clause power, and the Government has never argued otherwise.

This Court, moreover, consistently has recognized that the power to care for the mentally ill and, where necessary, the power "to protect the community from the dangerous tendencies of some" mentally ill persons, are among the numerous powers that remain with the States. As a consequence, we have held that States may "take measures to restrict the freedom of the dangerously mentally ill"—including those who are sexually dangerous—provided that such commitments satisfy due process and other constitutional requirements.

Section 4248 closely resembles the involuntary civil-commitment laws that States have enacted under their *parens patriae* and general police powers. To be sure, protecting society from violent sexual offenders is certainly an important end. Sexual abuse is a despicable act with untold consequences for the victim personally and society generally. But the Constitution does not vest in Congress the authority to protect society from every bad act that might befall it.

In my view, this should decide the question. Section 4248 runs afoul of our settled understanding of Congress' power under the Necessary and Proper Clause. Congress may act under that Clause only when its legislation "carr [ies] into Execution" one of the Federal Government's enumerated powers. Section 4248 does not execute *any* enumerated power. Section 4248 is therefore unconstitutional.

[II]

The Court perfunctorily genuflects to *McCulloch*'s framework for assessing Congress' Necessary and Proper Clause authority, and to the principle of dual sovereignty it helps to maintain, then promptly abandons both in favor of a novel five-factor test supporting its conclusion that § 4248 is a "'necessary and proper'" adjunct to a jumble of *unenumerated* "authorit [ies]." The Court's newly minted test cannot be reconciled with the Clause's plain text or with two centuries of our precedents interpreting it. It also raises more questions than it answers. Must each of the five considerations exist before the Court sustains future federal legislation as proper exercises of Congress' Necessary and Proper Clause authority? What if the facts of a given case support a finding of only four considerations? Or three? And if three or four will suffice, *which* three or four are imperative? At a minimum, this shift from the two-step *McCulloch* framework to this five-consideration approach warrants an explanation as to why *McCulloch* is no longer good enough and which of the five considerations will bear the most weight in future cases, assuming some number less than five suffices. (Or, if not, why all five are required.) The Court provides no answers to these questions.

* * *

Not long ago, this Court described the Necessary and Proper Clause as "the last, best hope of those who defend ultra vires congressional action." Regrettably, today's opinion breathes new life into that Clause, and the Court's protestations to the contrary notwithstanding—comes perilously close to transforming the Necessary and Proper Clause into a basis for the federal police power that "we *always* have rejected." In so doing, the Court endorses the precise abuse of power Article I is designed to prevent-the use of a limited grant of authority as a "pretext . . . for the accomplishment of objects not intrusted to the government."

D. Congress's Powers Under the Post-Civil War Amendments

2. What Is the Scope of Congress's Power? (casebook, p. 253)

Section 5 of the Voting Rights Act of 1965 requires that jurisdictions with a history of race discrimination in voting obtain "preclearance" from the Attorney General or a federal court before changes in their election practices. This was adopted pursuant to Section 2 of the Fifteenth Amendment, which authorizes Congress to enact laws to enforce the provisions of that Amendment, which prohibits denial of the right to vote on account of race or previous condition of servitude.

In 2006, Congress extended Section 5 of the Voting Rights Act for another 25 years. In *Northwest Austin Municipal Utility District Number One v. Holder*, the Court considered, but did not decide, whether it was constitutional for Congress to extend this law. The Court avoided the constitutional issue by allowing local districts to seek to "bail out" of the law and thus avoid its requirements. If jurisdictions are denied such bailouts, it is likely they will reassert that the statute is unconstitutional and the issue of the law's constitutionality will return to the Supreme Court.

NORTHWEST AUSTIN MUNICIPAL UTILITY DISTRICT
NUMBER ONE v. HOLDER
129 S.Ct. 2504 (2009)

Chief Justice ROBERTS delivered the opinion of the Court.

The plaintiff in this case is a small utility district raising a big question-the constitutionality of § 5 of the Voting Rights Act. The district has an elected board, and is required by § 5 to seek preclearance from federal authorities in Washington, D.C., before it can change anything about those elections. This is required even though there has never been any evidence of racial discrimination in voting in the district.

The district filed suit seeking relief from these preclearance obligations under the "bailout" provision of the Voting Rights Act. That provision allows the release of a "political subdivision" from the preclearance requirements if certain rigorous conditions are met. The court below denied relief, concluding that bailout was unavailable to a political subdivision like the utility district that did not register its own voters. The district appealed, arguing that the Act imposes no such limitation on bailout, and that if it does, the preclearance requirements are unconstitutional.

That constitutional question has attracted ardent briefs from dozens of interested parties, but the importance of the question does not justify our rushing to decide it. Quite the contrary: Our usual practice is to avoid the unnecessary resolution of constitutional questions. We agree that the district is eligible under the Act to seek bailout. We therefore reverse, and do not reach the constitutionality of § 5.

I

A

The Fifteenth Amendment promises that the "right of citizens of the United States to vote shall not be denied or abridged . . . on account of race, color, or previous condition of servitude." In addition to that self-executing right, the Amendment also gives Congress the "power to enforce this article by appropriate legislation." The first century of congressional enforcement of the Amendment, however, can only be regarded as a failure. Early enforcement Acts were inconsistently applied and repealed with the rise of Jim Crow. Another series of enforcement statutes in the 1950s and 1960s depended on individual lawsuits filed by the Department of Justice. But litigation is slow and expensive, and the States were creative in "contriving new rules" to continue violating the Fifteenth Amendment "in the face of adverse federal court decrees."

Congress responded with the Voting Rights Act. Section 2 of the Act operates nationwide; as it exists today, that provision forbids any "standard, practice, or procedure" that "results in a denial or abridgment of the right of any citizen of the United States to vote on account of race or color." Section 2 is not at issue in this case.

The remainder of the Act constitutes a "scheme of stringent remedies aimed at areas where voting discrimination has been most flagrant." Rather than continuing to depend on case-by-case litigation, the Act directly pre-empted the most powerful tools of black disenfranchisement in the covered areas. All literacy tests and similar voting qualifications were abolished by § 4 of the Act. Although such tests may have been facially neutral, they were easily manipulated to keep blacks from voting. The Act also empowered federal examiners to override state determinations about who was eligible to vote.

These two remedies were bolstered by § 5, which suspended all changes in state election procedure until they were submitted to and approved by a three-judge Federal District Court in Washington, D.C., or the Attorney General. Such preclearance is granted only if the change neither "has the purpose nor will have the effect of denying or abridging the right to vote on account of race or color." We have interpreted the requirements of § 5 to apply not only to the ballot-access rights guaranteed by § 4, but to drawing district lines as well.

To confine these remedies to areas of flagrant disenfranchisement, the Act applied them only to States that had used a forbidden test or device in November 1964, and had less than 50% voter registration or turnout in the 1964 Presidential election. Congress recognized that the coverage formula it had adopted "might bring within its sweep governmental units not guilty of any unlawful discriminatory voting practices." It therefore "afforded such jurisdictions immediately available protection in the form of . . . [a] 'bailout' suit."

To bail out under the current provision, a jurisdiction must seek a declaratory judgment from a three-judge District Court in Washington, D.C. It must show that for the previous 10 years it has not used any forbidden voting test, has not been subject to any valid objection under § 5, and has not been found liable for other voting rights violations; it must also show that it has "engaged in constructive efforts to eliminate intimidation and harassment" of voters, and similar measures. The Attorney General can consent to entry of judgment in favor of bailout if the evidence warrants it, though other interested parties are allowed to intervene in the declaratory judgment action. There are other restrictions: To bail out, a covered jurisdiction must show that every jurisdiction in its territory has complied with all of these requirements. The District Court also retains continuing jurisdiction over a successful bailout suit for 10 years, and may reinstate coverage if any violation is found.

As enacted, §§ 4 and 5 of the Voting Rights Act were temporary provisions. They were expected to be in effect for only five years. We upheld the temporary Voting Rights Act of 1965 as an appropriate exercise of congressional power in *Katzenbach v. South Carolina,* explaining that "[t]he constitutional propriety of the Voting Rights Act of 1965 must be judged with reference to the historical experience which it reflects." We concluded that the problems Congress faced when it passed the Act were so dire that "exceptional conditions [could] justify legislative measures not otherwise appropriate."

Congress reauthorized the Act in 1970 (for 5 years), 1975 (for 7 years), and 1982 (for 25 years). The coverage formula remained the same, based on the use of voting-eligibility tests and the rate of registration and turnout among all voters, but the pertinent dates for assessing these criteria moved from 1964 to include 1968 and eventually 1972. We upheld each of these reauthorizations against constitutional challenges, finding that circumstances continued to justify the provisions. Most recently, in 2006, Congress extended § 5 for yet another 25 years. The 2006 Act retained 1972 as the last baseline year for triggering coverage under § 5. It is that latest extension that is now before us.

B

Northwest Austin Municipal Utility District Number One was created in 1987 to deliver city services to residents of a portion of Travis County, Texas. It is governed by a board of five members, elected to staggered terms of four years. The district does not register voters but is responsible for its own elections; for administrative reasons, those elections are run by Travis County. Because the district is located in Texas, it is subject to the obligations of § 5, although there is no evidence that it has ever discriminated on the basis of race.

The district filed suit in the District Court for the District of Columbia, seeking relief under the statute's bailout provisions and arguing in the alternative that, if interpreted to render the district ineligible for bailout, § 5 was unconstitutional.

II

The historic accomplishments of the Voting Rights Act are undeniable. When it was first passed, unconstitutional discrimination was rampant and the "registration of voting-age whites ran roughly 50 percentage points or more ahead" of black registration in many covered States. Today, the registration gap between white and black voters is in single digits in the covered States; in some of those States, blacks now register and vote at higher rates than whites. Similar dramatic improvements have occurred for other racial minorities. "[M]any of the first generation barriers to minority voter registration and voter turnout that were in place prior to the [Voting Rights Act] have been eliminated."

At the same time, § 5, "which authorizes federal intrusion into sensitive areas of state and local policymaking, imposes substantial 'federalism costs.'" These federalism costs have caused Members of this Court to express serious misgivings about the constitutionality of § 5.

Section 5 goes beyond the prohibition of the Fifteenth Amendment by suspending *all* changes to state election law—however innocuous—until they have been precleared by federal authorities in Washington, D.C. The preclearance requirement applies broadly, and in particular to every political subdivision in a covered State, no matter how small.

Some of the conditions that we relied upon in upholding this statutory scheme have unquestionably improved. Things have changed in the South. Voter turnout and registration rates now approach parity. Blatantly discriminatory evasions of federal decrees are rare. And minority candidates hold office at unprecedented levels.

These improvements are no doubt due in significant part to the Voting Rights Act itself, and stand as a monument to its success. Past success alone, however, is not adequate justification to retain the preclearance requirements. It may be that these improvements are insufficient and that conditions continue to warrant preclearance under the Act. But the Act imposes current burdens and must be justified by current needs.

The Act also differentiates between the States, despite our historic tradition that all the States enjoy "equal sovereignty." Distinctions can be justified in some cases. "The doctrine of the equality of States ... does not bar ... remedies for *local* evils which have subsequently appeared." But a departure from the fundamental principle of equal sovereignty requires a showing that a statute's disparate geographic coverage is sufficiently related to the problem that it targets. These federalism concerns are underscored by the argument that the preclearance requirements in one State would be unconstitutional in another.

The evil that § 5 is meant to address may no longer be concentrated in the jurisdictions singled out for preclearance. The statute's coverage formula is based on data that is now more than 35 years old, and there is considerable evidence that it fails to account for current political conditions. For example, the racial gap in voter registration and turnout is lower in the States originally covered by § 5 than it is nationwide. Congress heard warnings from supporters of extending § 5 that the evidence in the record did not address "systematic differences between the covered and the non-covered areas of the United States[,] ... and, in fact, the evidence that is in the record suggests that there is more similarity than difference."

The parties do not agree on the standard to apply in deciding whether, in light of the foregoing concerns, Congress exceeded its Fifteenth Amendment enforcement power in extending the preclearance requirements. The district argues that "[t]here must be a congruence and proportionality between the injury to be prevented or remedied and the means adopted to that end"; the Federal Government asserts that it is enough that the legislation be a "rational means to effectuate the constitutional prohibition." That question has been extensively briefed in this case, but we need not resolve it. The Act's preclearance requirements and its coverage formula raise serious constitutional questions under either test.

In assessing those questions, we are keenly mindful of our institutional role. We fully appreciate that judging the constitutionality of an Act of Congress is "the gravest and most delicate duty that this Court is called on to perform." "The Congress is a coequal branch of government whose Members take the same oath we do to uphold the Constitution of the United States." The Fifteenth Amendment empowers "Congress," not the Court, to determine in the first instance what legislation is needed to enforce it. Congress amassed a sizable record in support of its decision to extend the preclearance requirements, a record the District Court determined "document[ed] contemporary racial discrimination in covered states." The District Court also found that the record "demonstrat[ed] that section 5 prevents discriminatory voting changes" by "quietly but effectively deterring discriminatory changes."

We will not shrink from our duty "as the bulwar[k] of a limited constitution against legislative encroachments," The Federalist No. 78, p. 526 (J. Cooke ed. 1961) (A. Hamilton), but "[i]t is a well-established principle governing the prudent exercise of this Court's jurisdiction that normally the Court will not decide a constitutional question if there is some other ground upon which to dispose of the case." Here, the district also raises a statutory claim that it is eligible to bail out under § § 4 and 5.

Justice Thomas argues that the principle of constitutional avoidance has no pertinence here. He contends that even if we resolve the district's statutory argument in its favor, we would still have to reach the constitutional question, because the district's statutory argument would not afford it all the relief it seeks.

We disagree. The district expressly describes its constitutional challenge to § 5 as being "in the alternative" to its statutory argument. We therefore turn to the district's statutory argument.

III

Section 4(b) of the Voting Rights Act authorizes a bailout suit by a "State or political subdivision." There is no dispute that the district is a political subdivision of the State of Texas in the ordinary sense of the term. The district was created under Texas law with "powers of government" relating to local utilities and natural resources.

The Act, however, also provides a narrower statutory definition in § 14 (c)(2): " '[P]olitical subdivision' shall mean any county or parish, except that where registration for voting is not conducted under the supervision of a county or parish, the term shall include any other subdivision of a State which conducts registration for voting." The District Court concluded that this definition applied to the bailout provision in § 4(a), and that the district did not qualify, since it is not a county or parish and does not conduct its own voter registration.

Were the scope of § 4(a) considered in isolation from the rest of the statute and our prior cases, the District Court's approach might well be correct. But here specific precedent, the structure of the Voting Rights Act, and underlying constitutional concerns compel a broader reading of the bailout provision. We hold that all political subdivisions—not only those described in § 14(c)(2)—are eligible to file a bailout suit.

More than 40 years ago, this Court concluded that "exceptional conditions" prevailing in certain parts of the country justified extraordinary legislation otherwise unfamiliar to our federal system. In part due to the success of that legislation, we are now a very different Nation. Whether conditions continue to justify such legislation is a difficult constitutional question we do not answer today. We conclude instead that the Voting Rights Act permits all political subdivisions, including the district in this case, to seek relief from its preclearance requirements.

Justice THOMAS, concurring in the judgment in part and dissenting in part.

This appeal presents two questions: first, whether appellant is entitled to bail out from coverage under the Voting Rights Act of 1965 (VRA); and second, whether the preclearance requirement of § 5 of the VRA is unconstitutional. Because the Court's statutory decision does not provide appellant with full relief, I conclude that it is inappropriate to apply the constitutional avoidance doctrine in this case. I would therefore decide the constitutional issue presented and hold that § 5 exceeds Congress' power to enforce the Fifteenth Amendment.

I

The doctrine of constitutional avoidance factors heavily in the Court's conclusion that appellant is eligible for bailout as a "political subdivision" under § 4(a) of the VRA. Regardless of the Court's resolution of the statutory question, I am in full agreement that this case raises serious questions concerning the constitutionality of § 5 of the VRA. But, unlike the Court, I do not believe that the doctrine of constitutional avoidance is applicable here. The ultimate relief sought in this case is not bailout eligibility—it is bailout itself.

Eligibility for bailout turns on the statutory question addressed by the Court—the proper definition of "political subdivision" in the bailout clauses of § 4(a) of the VRA. Entitlement to bailout, however, requires a covered "political subdivision" to submit substantial evidence indicating that it is not engaging in "discrimination in voting on account of race." The Court properly declines to give appellant bailout because appellant has not yet proved its compliance with the statutory requirements for such relief. In fact, the record below shows that appellant's factual entitlement to bailout is a vigorously contested issue. Given its resolution of the statutory question, the Court has thus correctly remanded the case for resolution of appellant's factual entitlement to bailout.

But because the Court is not in a position to award appellant bailout, adjudication of the constitutionality of § 5, in my view, cannot be avoided. "Traditionally, the avoidance canon was not a doctrine under which courts read statutes to avoid mere constitutional doubts. Instead, it commanded courts, when faced with two plausible constructions of a statute—one constitutional and the other unconstitutional—to choose the constitutional reading." To the extent that constitutional avoidance is a worthwhile tool of statutory construction, it is because it allows a court to dispose of an entire case on grounds that do not require the court to pass on a statute's constitutionality. Absent a determination that appellant is not just eligible for bailout, but is entitled to it, this case will not have been entirely disposed of on a nonconstitutional ground. Invocation of the doctrine of constitutional avoidance is therefore inappropriate in this case.

The doctrine of constitutional avoidance is also unavailable here because an interpretation of § 4(a) that merely makes more political subdivisions *eligible* for bailout does not render § 5 constitutional and the Court notably does not suggest otherwise. Bailout eligibility is a distant prospect for most covered jurisdictions.

II

The Court quite properly alerts Congress that § 5 tests the outer boundaries of its Fifteenth Amendment enforcement authority and may not be constitutional. And, although I respect the Court's careful approach to this weighty issue, In evertheless believe it is necessary to definitively resolve that important question. For the reasons set forth below, I conclude that the lack of current evidence of intentional discrimination with respect to voting renders § 5 unconstitutional. The provision can no longer be justified as an appropriate mechanism for enforcement of the Fifteenth Amendment.

The extensive pattern of discrimination that led the Court to previously uphold § 5 as enforcing the Fifteenth Amendment no longer exists. Covered jurisdictions are not now engaged in a systematic campaign to deny black citizens access to the ballot through intimidation and violence. And the days of "grandfather clauses, property qualifications, 'good character' tests, and the requirement that registrants 'understand' or 'interpret' certain matter," are gone. There is thus currently no concerted effort in these jurisdictions to engage in the "unremitting and ingenious defiance of the Constitution," that served as the constitutional basis for upholding the "uncommon exercise of congressional power" embodied in § 5.

The lack of sufficient evidence that the covered jurisdictions currently engage in the type of discrimination that underlay the enactment of § 5 undermines any basis for retaining it. Punishment for long past sins is not a legitimate basis for imposing a forward-looking preventative measure that has already served its purpose. Those supporting § 5's reenactment argue that without it these jurisdictions would return to the racially discriminatory practices of 30 and 40 years ago. But there is no evidence that public officials stand ready, if given the chance, to again engage in concerted acts of violence, terror, and subterfuge in order to keep minorities from voting. Without such evidence, the charge can only be premised on outdated assumptions about racial attitudes in the covered jurisdictions. Admitting that a prophylactic law as broad as § 5 is no longer constitutionally justified based on current evidence of discrimination is not a sign of defeat. It is an acknowledgment of victory.

The current statistical evidence confirms that the emergency that prompted the enactment of § 5 has long since passed. By 2006, the voter registration rates for blacks in Alabama, Louisiana, and Mississippi had jumped to 71.8%, 66.9%, and 72.2%, respectively. Therefore, in contrast to the *Katzenbach* Court's finding that the "registration of voting-age whites ran roughly 50 percentage points or more ahead of Negro registration" in these States in 1964, since that time this disparity has nearly vanished. In 2006, the disparity was only 3 percentage points in Alabama, 8 percentage points in Louisiana, and in Mississippi, black voter registration actually exceeded white voter registration by 1.5 percentage points. In addition, blacks in these three covered States also have higher registration numbers than the registration rate for whites in noncovered states.

Indeed, when reenacting § 5 in 2006, Congress evidently understood that the emergency conditions which prompted § 5's original enactment no longer exist. Instead of relying on the kind of evidence that the *Katzenbach* Court had found so persuasive, Congress instead based reenactment on evidence of what it termed "second generation barriers constructed to prevent minority voters from fully participating in the electoral process." But such evidence is not probative of the type of purposeful discrimination that prompted Congress to enact § 5 in 1965. For example, Congress relied upon evidence of racially polarized voting within the covered jurisdictions. But racially polarized voting is not evidence of unconstitutional discrimination, is not state action, and is not a problem unique to the South.

This is not to say that voter discrimination is extinct. Indeed, the District Court singled out a handful of examples of allegedly discriminatory voting practices from the record made by Congress. But the existence of discrete and isolated incidents of interference with the right to vote has never been sufficient justification for the imposition of § 5's extraordinary requirements. From its inception, the statute was promoted as a measure needed to neutralize a coordinated and unrelenting campaign to deny an entire race access to the ballot. Perfect compliance with the Fifteenth Amendment's substantive command is not now—nor has it ever been—the yardstick for determining whether Congress has the power to employ broad prophylactic legislation to enforce that Amendment. The burden remains with Congress to prove that the extreme circumstances warranting § 5's enactment persist today. A record of scattered infringement of the right to vote is not a constitutionally acceptable substitute.

In 1870, the Fifteenth Amendment was ratified in order to guarantee that no citizen would be denied the right to vote based on race, color, or previous condition of servitude. Congress passed § 5 of the VRA in 1965 because that promise had remained unfulfilled for far too long. But now—more than 40 years later—the violence, intimidation, and subterfuge that led Congress to pass § 5 and this Court to uphold it no longer remains. An acknowledgment of § 5's unconstitutionality represents a fulfillment of the Fifteenth Amendment's promise of full enfranchisement and honors the success achieved by the VRA.

Chapter 3

The Federal Executive Power

C. The Constitutional Problems of the Administrative State

3. Checking administrative power (casebook, p. 355)

In *Free Enterprise Fund v. Public Company Accountability Oversight Board* (2010), the Court considered the appointment and removal power. In reading the case, it is also important to contrast the difference between the majority and the dissent in their approach to separation of powers.

FREE ENTERPRISE FUND v. PUBLIC COMPANY
ACCOUNTING OVERSIGHT BOARD
130 S.Ct. _____ (2010)

Chief Justice ROBERTS delivered the opinion of the Court.

Our Constitution divided the "powers of the new Federal Government into three defined categories, Legislative, Executive, and Judicial." Article II vests "[t]he executive Power . . . in a President of the United States of America," who must "take Care that the Laws be faithfully executed." In light of "[t]he impossibility that one man should be able to perform all the great business of the State," the Constitution provides for executive officers to "assist the supreme Magistrate in discharging the duties of his trust."

Since 1789, the Constitution has been understood to empower the President to keep these officers accountable-by removing them from office, if necessary. This Court has determined, however, that this authority is not without limit. In *Humphrey's Executor v. United States* (1935), we held that Congress can, under certain circumstances, create independent agencies run by principal officers appointed by the President, whom the President may not remove at will but only for good cause. Likewise, in *United States v. Perkins* (1886), and *Morrison v. Olson* (1988), the Court sustained similar restrictions on the power of principal executive officers-themselves responsible to the President-to remove their own inferiors. The parties do not ask us to reexamine any of these precedents, and we do not do so.

We are asked, however, to consider a new situation not yet encountered by the Court. The question is whether these separate layers of protection may be combined. May the President be restricted in his ability to remove a principal officer, who is in turn restricted in his ability to remove an inferior officer, even though that inferior officer determines the policy and enforces the laws of the United States?

We hold that such multilevel protection from removal is contrary to Article II's vesting of the executive power in the President. The President cannot "take Care that the Laws be faithfully executed" if he cannot oversee the faithfulness of the officers who execute them. Here the President cannot remove an officer who enjoys more than one level of good-cause protection, even if the President determines that the officer is neglecting his duties or discharging them improperly. That judgment is instead committed to another officer, who may or may not agree with the President's determination, and whom the President cannot remove simply because that officer disagrees with him. This contravenes the President's "constitutional obligation to ensure the faithful execution of the laws."

I

After a series of celebrated accounting debacles, Congress enacted the Sarbanes-Oxley Act of 2002 (or Act). Among other measures, the Act introduced tighter regulation of the accounting industry under a new Public Company Accounting Oversight Board. The Board is composed of five members, appointed to staggered 5-year terms by the Securities and Exchange Commission. It was modeled on private self-regulatory organizations in the securities industry—such as the New York Stock Exchange—that investigate and discipline their own members subject to Commission oversight. Congress created the Board as a private "nonprofit corporation," and Board members and employees are not considered Government "officer[s] or employee[s]" for statutory purposes. The Board can thus recruit its members and employees from the private sector by paying salaries far above the standard Government pay scale.[1]

---

1. The current salary for the Chairman is $673,000. Other Board members receive $547,000. [Footnote by the Court.]

Unlike the self-regulatory organizations, however, the Board is a Government-created, Government-appointed entity, with expansive powers to govern an entire industry. Every accounting firm—both foreign and domestic—that participates in auditing public companies under the securities laws must register with the Board, pay it an annual fee, and comply with its rules and oversight. The Board is charged with enforcing the Sarbanes-Oxley Act, the securities laws, the Commission's rules, its own rules, and professional accounting standards. To this end, the Board may regulate every detail of an accounting firm's practice, including hiring and professional development, promotion, supervision of audit work, the acceptance of new business and the continuation of old, internal inspection procedures, professional ethics rules, and "such other requirements as the Board may prescribe."

The Board promulgates auditing and ethics standards, performs routine inspections of all accounting firms, demands documents and testimony, and initiates formal investigations and disciplinary proceedings. The willful violation of any Board rule is treated as a willful violation of the Securities Exchange Act of 1934, a federal crime punishable by up to 20 years' imprisonment or $25 million in fines ($5 million for a natural person). And the Board itself can issue severe sanctions in its disciplinary proceedings, up to and including the permanent revocation of a firm's registration, a permanent ban on a person's associating with any registered firm, and money penalties of $15 million ($750,000 for a natural person). Despite the provisions specifying that Board members are not Government officials for statutory purposes, the parties agree that the Board is "part of the Government" for constitutional purposes, and that its members are "'Officers of the United States'" who "exercis[e] significant authority pursuant to the laws of the United States."

The Act places the Board under the SEC's oversight, particularly with respect to the issuance of rules or the imposition of sanctions (both of which are subject to Commission approval and alteration). But the individual members of the Board—like the officers and directors of the self-regulatory organizations—are substantially insulated from the Commission's control. The Commission cannot remove Board members at will, but only "for good cause shown," "in accordance with" certain procedures.

Those procedures require a Commission finding, "on the record" and "after notice and opportunity for a hearing," that the Board member "(A) has willfully violated any provision of th[e] Act, the rules of the Board, or the securities laws; (B) has willfully abused the authority of that member; or (C) without reasonable justification or excuse, has failed to enforce compliance with any such provision or rule, or any professional standard by any registered public accounting firm or any associated person thereof." Removal of a Board member requires a formal Commission order and is subject to judicial review. The parties agree that the Commissioners cannot themselves be removed by the President except under the *Humphrey's Executor* standard of "inefficiency, neglect of duty, or malfeasance in office."

[II]

We hold that the dual for-cause limitations on the removal of Board members contravene the Constitution's separation of powers.

The Constitution provides that "[t]he executive Power shall be vested in a President of the United States of America." As Madison stated on the floor of the First Congress, "if any power whatsoever is in its nature Executive, it is the power of appointing, overseeing, and controlling those who execute the laws."

The landmark case of *Myers v. United States* reaffirmed the principle that Article II confers on the President "the general administrative control of those executing the laws." It is *his* responsibility to take care that the laws be faithfully executed. The buck stops with the President, in Harry Truman's famous phrase. As we explained in *Myers,* the President therefore must have some "power of removing those for whom he can not continue to be responsible."

Nearly a decade later in *Humphrey's Executor,* this Court held that *Myers* did not prevent Congress from conferring good-cause tenure on the principal officers of certain independent agencies. That case concerned the members of the Federal Trade Commission, who held 7-year terms and could not be removed by the President except for "'inefficiency, neglect of duty, or malfeasance in office.'" The Court distinguished *Myers* on the ground that *Myers* concerned "an officer [who] is merely one of the units in the executive department and, hence, inherently subject to the exclusive and illimitable power of removal by the Chief Executive, whose subordinate and aid he is." By contrast, the Court characterized the FTC as "quasi-legislative and quasi-judicial" rather than "purely executive," and held that Congress could require it "to act . . . independently of executive control." Because "one who holds his office only during the pleasure of another, cannot be depended upon to maintain an attitude of independence against the latter's will," the Court held that Congress had power to "fix the period during which [the Commissioners] shall continue in office, and to forbid their removal except for cause in the meantime."

Humphrey's Executor did not address the removal of inferior officers, whose appointment Congress may vest in heads of departments. If Congress does so, it is ordinarily the department head, rather than the President, who enjoys the power of removal. This Court has upheld for-cause limitations on that power as well.

As explained, we have previously upheld limited restrictions on the President's removal power. In those cases, however, only one level of protected tenure separated the President from an officer exercising executive power. It was the President—or a subordinate he could remove at will—who decided whether the officer's conduct merited removal under the good-cause standard.

The Act before us does something quite different. It not only protects Board members from removal except for good cause, but withdraws from the President any decision on whether that good cause exists. That decision is vested instead in other tenured officers—the Commissioners—none of whom is subject to the President's direct control. The result is a Board that is not accountable to the President, and a President who is not responsible for the Board.

The added layer of tenure protection makes a difference. Without a layer of insulation between the Commission and the Board, the Commission could remove a Board member at any time, and therefore would be fully responsible for what the Board does. The President could then hold the Commission to account for its supervision of the Board, to the same extent that he may hold the Commission to account for everything else it does.

A second level of tenure protection changes the nature of the President's review. Now the Commission cannot remove a Board member at will. The President therefore cannot hold the Commission fully accountable for the Board's conduct, to the same extent that he may hold the Commission accountable for everything else that it does. The Commissioners are not responsible for the Board's actions. They are only responsible for their own determination of whether the Act's rigorous good-cause standard is met. And even if the President disagrees with their determination, he is powerless to intervene-unless that determination is so unreasonable as to constitute "inefficiency, neglect of duty, or malfeasance in office."

This novel structure does not merely add to the Board's independence, but transforms it. Neither the President, nor anyone directly responsible to him, nor even an officer whose conduct he may review only for good cause, has full control over the Board. The President is stripped of the power our precedents have preserved, and his ability to execute the laws—by holding his subordinates accountable for their conduct—is impaired.

That arrangement is contrary to Article II's vesting of the executive power in the President. Without the ability to oversee the Board, or to attribute the Board's failings to those whom he *can* oversee, the President is no longer the judge of the Board's conduct. He is not the one who decides whether Board members are abusing their offices or neglecting their duties. He can neither ensure that the laws are faithfully executed, nor be held responsible for a Board member's breach of faith. This violates the basic principle that the President "cannot delegate ultimate responsibility or the active obligation to supervise that goes with it," because Article II "makes a single President responsible for the actions of the Executive Branch."

Indeed, if allowed to stand, this dispersion of responsibility could be multiplied. If Congress can shelter the bureaucracy behind two layers of good-cause tenure, why not a third? At oral argument, the Government was unwilling to concede that even *five* layers between the President and the Board would be too many. The officers of such an agency—safely encased within a Matryoshka doll of tenure protections—would be immune from Presidential oversight, even as they exercised power in the people's name.

The diffusion of power carries with it a diffusion of accountability. The people do not vote for the "Officers of the United States." They instead look to the President to guide the "assistants or deputies . . . subject to his superintendence." Without a clear and effective chain of command, the public cannot "determine on whom the blame or the punishment of a pernicious measure, or series of pernicious measures ought really to fall." That is why the Framers sought to ensure that "those who are employed in the execution of the law will be in their proper situation, and the chain of dependence be preserved; the lowest officers, the middle grade, and the highest, will depend, as they ought, on the President, and the President on the community."

By granting the Board executive power without the Executive's oversight, this Act subverts the President's ability to ensure that the laws are faithfully executed—as well as the public's ability to pass judgment on his efforts. The Act's restrictions are incompatible with the Constitution's separation of powers.

Respondents and the dissent resist this conclusion, portraying the Board as "the kind of practical accommodation between the Legislature and the Executive that should be permitted in a 'workable government.'" No one doubts Congress's power to create a vast and varied federal bureaucracy. But where, in all this, is the role for oversight by an elected President? The Constitution requires that a President chosen by the entire Nation oversee the execution of the laws. And the "'fact that a given law or procedure is efficient, convenient, and useful in facilitating functions of government, standing alone, will not save it if it is contrary to the Constitution,'" for "'[c]onvenience and efficiency are not the primary objectives-or the hallmarks-of democratic government.'"

One can have a government that functions without being ruled by functionaries, and a government that benefits from expertise without being ruled by experts. Our Constitution was adopted to enable the people to govern themselves, through their elected leaders. The growth of the Executive Branch, which now wields vast power and touches almost every aspect of daily life, heightens the concern that it may slip from the Executive's control, and thus from that of the people. This concern is largely absent from the dissent's paean to the administrative state.

Calls to abandon those protections in light of "the era's perceived necessity," are not unusual. Nor is the argument from bureaucratic expertise limited only to the field of accounting. The failures of accounting regulation may be a "pressing national problem," but "a judiciary that licensed extraconstitutional government with each issue of comparable gravity would, in the long run, be far worse." Neither respondents nor the dissent explains why the Board's task, unlike so many others, requires *more* than one layer of insulation from the President—or, for that matter, why only two. The point is not to take issue with for-cause limitations in general; we do not do that. The question here is far more modest. We deal with the unusual situation, never before addressed by the Court, of two layers of for-cause tenure. And though it may be criticized as "elementary arithmetical logic," two layers are not the same as one.

[III]

[P]etitioners argue that Board members are principal officers requiring Presidential appointment with the Senate's advice and consent. We held in *Edmond v. United States,* (1997), that "[w]hether one is an 'inferior' officer depends on whether he has a superior," and that "'inferior officers' are officers whose work is directed and supervised at some level" by other officers appointed by the President with the Senate's consent. In particular, we noted that "[t]he power to remove officers" at will and without cause "is a powerful tool for control" of an inferior. As explained above, the statutory restrictions on the Commission's power to remove Board members are unconstitutional and void. Given that the Commission is properly viewed, under the Constitution, as possessing the power to remove Board members at will, and given the Commission's other oversight authority, we have no hesitation in concluding that the Board members are inferior officers whose appointment Congress may permissibly vest in a "Hea[d] of Departmen[t]."

In light of the foregoing, petitioners are not entitled to broad injunctive relief against the Board's continued operations. But they are entitled to declaratory relief sufficient to ensure that the reporting requirements and auditing standards to which they are subject will be enforced only by a constitutional agency accountable to the Executive.

* * *

The Constitution that makes the President accountable to the people for executing the laws also gives him the power to do so. That power includes, as a general matter, the authority to remove those who assist him in carrying out his duties. Without such power, the President could not be held fully accountable for discharging his own responsibilities; the buck would stop somewhere else. Such diffusion of authority "would greatly diminish the intended and necessary responsibility of the chief magistrate himself."

While we have sustained in certain cases limits on the President's removal power, the Act before us imposes a new type of restriction—two levels of protection from removal for those who nonetheless exercise significant executive power. Congress cannot limit the President's authority in this way.

Justice BREYER, with whom Justice STEVENS, Justice GINSBURG, and Justice SOTOMAYOR join, dissenting.

The Court holds unconstitutional a statute providing that the Securities and Exchange Commission can remove members of the Public Company Accounting Oversight Board from office only for cause. It argues that granting the "inferior officer[s]" on the Accounting Board "more than one level of good-cause protection . . . contravenes the President's 'constitutional obligation to ensure the faithful execution of the laws.'" I agree that the Accounting Board members are inferior officers. But in my view the statute does not significantly interfere with the President's "executive Power." It violates no separation-of-powers principle. And the Court's contrary holding threatens to disrupt severely the fair and efficient administration of the laws. I consequently dissent.

I

In answering the question presented, we cannot look to more specific constitutional text, such as the text of the Appointments Clause or the Presentment Clause, upon which the Court has relied in other separation-of-powers cases. That is because, with the exception of the general "vesting" and "take care" language, the Constitution is completely "silent with respect to the power of removal from office."

Nor does history offer significant help. The President's power to remove Executive Branch officers "was not discussed in the Constitutional Convention." Nor does this Court's precedent fully answer the question presented. At least it does not clearly invalidate the provision in dispute.

In short, the question presented lies at the intersection of two sets of conflicting, broadly framed constitutional principles. And no text, no history, perhaps no precedent provides any clear answer.

When previously deciding this kind of nontextual question, the Court has emphasized the importance of examining how a particular provision, taken in context, is likely to function. It is not surprising that the Court in these circumstances has looked to function and context, and not to bright-line rules. For one thing, that approach embodies the intent of the Framers.

For another, a functional approach permits Congress and the President the flexibility needed to adapt statutory law to changing circumstances. That is why the "powers conferred upon the Federal Government by the Constitution were phrased in language broad enough to allow for the expansion of the Federal Government's role" over time. Indeed, the Federal Government at the time of the founding consisted of about 2,000 employees and served a population of about 4 million. Today, however, the Federal Government employs about *4.4 million workers* who serve a Nation of more than 310 million people living in a society characterized by rapid technological, economic, and social change.

The upshot is that today vast numbers of statutes governing vast numbers of subjects, concerned with vast numbers of different problems, provide for, or foresee, their execution or administration through the work of administrators organized within many different kinds of administrative structures, exercising different kinds of administrative authority, to achieve their legislatively mandated objectives. And, given the nature of the Government's work, it is not surprising that administrative units come in many different shapes and sizes.

These practical reasons not only support our precedents' determination that cases such as this should examine the specific functions and context at issue; they also indicate that judges should hesitate before second-guessing a "for cause" decision made by the other branches. Compared to Congress and the President, the Judiciary possesses an inferior understanding of the realities of administration, and the manner in which power, including and most especially political power, operates in context.

There is no indication that the two comparatively more expert branches were divided in their support for the "for cause" provision at issue here. In this case, the Act embodying the provision was passed by a vote of 423 to 3 in the House of Representatives and a by vote of 99 to 0 in the Senate. The creation of the Accounting Board was discussed at great length in both bodies without anyone finding in its structure any constitutional problem. The President signed the Act. And, when he did so, he issued a signing statement that critiqued multiple provisions of the Act but did not express any separation-of-powers concerns.

Thus, here, as in similar cases, we should decide the constitutional question in light of the provision's practical functioning in context. And our decision should take account of the Judiciary's comparative lack of institutional expertise.

II

[N]otwithstanding the majority's assertion that the removal authority is "*the* key" mechanism by which the President oversees inferior officers in the independent agencies, it appears that no President has ever actually sought to exercise that power by testing the scope of a "for cause" provision. But even if we put all these other matters to the side, we should still conclude that the "for cause" restriction before us will not restrict presidential power significantly. For one thing, the restriction directly limits, not the President's power, but the power of an already independent agency. The Court seems to have forgotten that fact when it identifies its central constitutional problem: According to the Court, the President "is powerless to intervene" if he has determined that the Board members' "conduct merit[s] removal" because "[t]hat decision is vested instead in other tenured officers—the Commissioners—none of whom is subject to the President's direct control." But so long as the President is *legitimately* foreclosed from removing the *Commissioners* except for cause (as the majority assumes), nullifying the Commission's power to remove Board members only for cause will not resolve the problem the Court has identified: The President will *still* be "powerless to intervene" by removing the Board members if the Commission reasonably decides not to do so.

In other words, the Court fails to show why *two* layers of "for cause" protection—Layer One insulating the Commissioners from the President, and Layer Two insulating the Board from the Commissioners—impose any more serious limitation upon the *President's* powers than *one* layer. Consider the four scenarios that might arise:

1. The President and the Commission both want to keep a Board member in office. Neither layer is relevant.
2. The President and the Commission both want to dismiss a Board member. Layer Two stops them both from doing so without cause. The President's ability to remove the Commission (Layer One) is irrelevant, for he and the Commission are in agreement.
3. The President wants to dismiss a Board member, but the Commission wants to keep the member. Layer One allows the Commission to make that determination notwithstanding the President's contrary view. Layer Two is irrelevant because the Commission does not seek to remove the Board member.
4. The President wants to keep a Board member, but the Commission wants to dismiss the Board member. Here, Layer Two *helps the President,* for it hinders the Commission's ability to dismiss a Board member whom the President wants to keep in place.

Thus, the majority's decision to eliminate only *Layer Two* accomplishes virtually nothing. And that is because a removal restriction's effect upon presidential power depends not on the presence of a "double-layer" of for-cause removal, as the majority pretends, but rather on the real-world nature of the President's relationship with the Commission. If the President confronts a Commission that seeks to *resist* his policy preferences—a distinct possibility when, as here, a Commission's membership must reflect both political parties, the restriction on the *Commission's* ability to remove a Board member is either irrelevant (as in scenario 3) or may actually help the President (as in scenario 4). And if the President faces a Commission that seeks to *implement* his policy preferences, Layer One is irrelevant, for the President and Commission see eye to eye.

But once we leave the realm of hypothetical logic and view the removal provision at issue in the context of the entire Act, its lack of practical effect becomes readily apparent. That is because the statute provides the Commission with full authority and virtually comprehensive control over all of the Board's functions. Those who created the Accounting Board modeled it, in terms of structure and authority, upon the semiprivate regulatory bodies prevalent in the area of financial regulation, such as the New York Stock Exchange and other similar self-regulating organizations.

What is left? The Commission's inability to remove a Board member whose perfectly *reasonable* actions cause the Commission to overrule him with great frequency? What is the practical likelihood of that occurring, or, if it does, of the President's serious concern about such a matter? Everyone concedes that the President's control over the Commission is constitutionally sufficient. And if the President's control over the Commission is sufficient, and the Commission's control over the Board is virtually absolute, then, as a practical matter, the President's control over the Board should prove sufficient as well.

At the same time, Congress and the President had good reason for enacting the challenged "for cause" provision. First and foremost, the Board adjudicates cases. This Court has long recognized the appropriateness of using "for cause" provisions to protect the personal independence of those who even only sometimes engage in adjudicatory functions.

Moreover, in addition to their adjudicative functions, the Accounting Board members supervise, and are themselves, technical professional experts. This Court has recognized that the "difficulties involved in the preparation of" sound auditing reports require the application of "scientific accounting principles." And this Court has recognized the constitutional legitimacy of a justification that rests agency independence upon the need for technical expertise. Here, the justification for insulating the "technical experts" on the Board from fear of losing their jobs due to political influence is particularly strong. Congress deliberately sought to provide that kind of protection.

We should ask one further question. Even if the "for cause" provision before us does not itself significantly interfere with the President's authority or aggrandize Congress' power, is it nonetheless necessary to adopt a bright-line rule forbidding the provision lest, through a series of such provisions, each itself upheld as reasonable, Congress might undercut the President's central constitutional role? The answer to this question is that no such need has been shown. Moreover, insofar as the Court seeks to create such a rule, it fails. And in failing it threatens a harm that is far more serious than any imaginable harm this "for cause" provision might bring about.

The Court begins to reveal the practical problems inherent in its double for-cause rule when it suggests that its rule may not apply to "the civil service." But even if I assume that the majority categorically excludes the competitive service from the scope of its new rule, the exclusion would be insufficient. Reading the criteria above as stringently as possible, I still see no way to avoid sweeping hundreds, perhaps thousands of high level government officials within the scope of the Court's holding, putting their job security and their administrative actions and decisions constitutionally at risk. To make even a conservative estimate, one would have to begin by listing federal departments, offices, bureaus and other agencies whose heads are by statute removable only "for cause." I have found 48 such agencies. Then it would be necessary to identify the senior officials in those agencies (just below the top) who themselves are removable only "for cause." I have identified 573 such high-ranking officials. This list is a conservative estimate because it consists only of career appointees in the Senior Executive Service (SES). The potential list of those whom today's decision affects is yet larger. [A]dministrative law judges (ALJs) "are all executive officers." My research reflects that the Federal Government relies on 1,584 ALJs to adjudicate administrative matters in over 25 agencies.

And what about the military? Commissioned military officers "are 'inferior officers.'" There are over 210,000 active-duty commissioned officers currently serving in the armed forces. And such officers can generally be so removed only by *other* commissioned officers, who themselves enjoy the same career protections.

Thus, notwithstanding the majority's assertions to the contrary, the potential consequences of today's holding are worrying. The upshot, I believe, is a legal dilemma. To interpret the Court's decision as applicable only in a few circumstances will make the rule less harmful but arbitrary. To interpret the rule more broadly will make the rule more rational, but destructive.

* * *

In my view the Court's decision is wrong-very wrong. Its rule of decision is both imprecise and overly broad. In light of the present imprecision, it must either narrow its rule arbitrarily, leaving it to apply virtually alone to the Accounting Board, or it will have to leave in place a broader rule of decision applicable to many other "inferior officers" as well. In doing the latter, it will undermine the President's authority. And it will create an obstacle, indeed pose a serious threat, to the proper functioning of that workable Government that the Constitution seeks to create—in provisions this Court is sworn to uphold.

Chapter 4

Limits on State Regulatory and Taxing Power

A. Preemption of State and Local Laws

2. Implied Preemption

a. Conflicts Preemption (casebook, p. 443)

If federal law and state law conflict, such as if they are mutually exclusive, then the state law is preempted. But this inevitably raises the question of whether the federal law is the minimum of regulation and states can go further, or if it is the maximum of regulation and states cannot add to it. This is the question in *Wyeth v. Levine*, which raised the issue of whether approval of a prescription drug warning label precluded state tort liability on a failure-to-warn theory.

WYETH v. LEVINE

129 S.Ct. 1187 (2009)

Justice STEVENS delivered the opinion of the Court.

Directly injecting the drug Phenergan into a patient's vein creates a significant risk of catastrophic consequences. A Vermont jury found that petitioner Wyeth, the manufacturer of the drug, had failed to provide an adequate warning of that risk and awarded damages to respondent Diana Levine to compensate her for the amputation of her arm. The warnings on Phenergan's label had been deemed sufficient by the federal Food and Drug Administration (FDA) when it approved Wyeth's new drug application in 1955 and when it later approved changes in the drug's labeling. The question we must decide is whether the FDA's approvals provide Wyeth with a complete defense to Levine's tort claims. We conclude that they do not.

I

Phenergan is Wyeth's brand name for promethazine hydrochloride, an antihistamine used to treat nausea. The injectable form of Phenergan can be administered intramuscularly or intravenously, and it can be administered intravenously through either the "IV-push" method, whereby the drug is injected directly into a patient's vein, or the "IV-drip" method, whereby the drug is introduced into a saline solution in a hanging intravenous bag and slowly descends through a catheter inserted in a patient's vein. The drug is corrosive and causes irreversible gangrene if it enters a patient's artery.

Levine's injury resulted from an IV-push injection of Phenergan. On April 7, 2000, as on previous visits to her local clinic for treatment of a migraine headache, she received an intramuscular injection of Demerol for her headache and Phenergan for her nausea. Because the combination did not provide relief, she returned later that day and received a second injection of both drugs. This time, the physician assistant administered the drugs by the IV-push method, and Phenergan entered Levine's artery, either because the needle penetrated an artery directly or because the drug escaped from the vein into surrounding tissue (a phenomenon called "perivascular extravasation") where it came in contact with arterial blood. As a result, Levine developed gangrene, and doctors amputated first her right hand and then her entire forearm. In addition to her pain and suffering, Levine incurred substantial medical expenses and the loss of her livelihood as a professional musician.

After settling claims against the health center and clinician, Levine brought an action for damages against Wyeth, relying on common-law negligence and strict-liability theories. Although Phenergan's labeling warned of the danger of gangrene and amputation following inadvertent intra-arterial injection, Levine alleged that the labeling was defective because it failed to instruct clinicians to use the IV-drip method of intravenous administration instead of the higher risk IV-push method. More broadly, she alleged that Phenergan is not reasonably safe for intravenous administration because the foreseeable risks of gangrene and loss of limb are great in relation to the drug's therapeutic benefits.

Wyeth filed a motion for summary judgment, arguing that Levine's failure-to-warn claims were pre-empted by federal law. The court found no merit in Wyeth's pre-emption argument. Answering questions on a special verdict form, the jury found that Wyeth was negligent, that Phenergan was a defective product as a result of inadequate warnings and instructions, and that no intervening cause had broken the causal connection between the product defects and the plaintiff's injury. It awarded total damages of $7,400,000, which the court reduced to account for Levine's earlier settlement with the health center and clinician. The Vermont Supreme Court affirmed.

II

Wyeth makes two separate pre-emption arguments: first, that it would have been impossible for it to comply with the state-law duty to modify Phenergan's labeling without violating federal law, and second, that recognition of Levine's state tort action creates an unacceptable "obstacle to the accomplishment and execution of the full purposes and objectives of Congress," because it substitutes a lay jury's decision about drug labeling for the expert judgment of the FDA. As a preface to our evaluation of these arguments, we identify two factual propositions decided during the trial court proceedings, emphasize two legal principles that guide our analysis, and review the history of the controlling federal statute.

The trial court proceedings established that Levine's injury would not have occurred if Phenergan's label had included an adequate warning about the risks of the IV-push method of administering the drug. The record contains evidence that the physician assistant administered a greater dose than the label prescribed, that she may have inadvertently injected the drug into an artery rather than a vein, and that she continued to inject the drug after Levine complained of pain. Nevertheless, the jury rejected Wyeth's argument that the clinician's conduct was an intervening cause that absolved it of liability. In finding Wyeth negligent as well as strictly liable, the jury also determined that Levine's injury was foreseeable. That the inadequate label was both a but-for and proximate cause of Levine's injury is supported by the record and no longer challenged by Wyeth.

The trial court proceedings further established that the critical defect in Phenergan's label was the lack of an adequate warning about the risks of IV-push administration. But, as the Vermont Supreme Court explained, the jury verdict established only that Phenergan's warning was insufficient. It did not mandate a particular replacement warning, nor did it require contraindicating IV-push administration: We therefore need not decide whether a state rule proscribing intravenous administration would be pre-empted. The narrower question presented is whether federal law pre-empts Levine's claim that Phenergan's label did not contain an adequate warning about using the IV-push method of administration.

Our answer to that question must be guided by two cornerstones of our pre-emption jurisprudence. First, "the purpose of Congress is the ultimate touchstone in every pre-emption case." Second, "[i]n all pre-emption cases, and particularly in those in which Congress has 'legislated . . . in a field which the States have traditionally occupied,' . . . we 'start with the assumption that the historic police powers of the States were not to be superseded by the Federal Act unless that was the clear and manifest purpose of Congress.'"

III

Wyeth first argues that Levine's state-law claims are pre-empted because it is impossible for it to comply with both the state-law duties underlying those claims and its federal labeling duties. The FDA's premarket approval of a new drug application includes the approval of the exact text in the proposed label. Generally speaking, a manufacturer may only change a drug label after the FDA approves a supplemental application. There is, however, an FDA regulation that permits a manufacturer to make certain changes to its label before receiving the agency's approval. Among other things, this "changes being effected" (CBE) regulation provides that if a manufacturer is changing a label to "add or strengthen a contraindication, warning, precaution, or adverse reaction" or to "add or strengthen an instruction about dosage and administration that is intended to increase the safe use of the drug product," it may make the labeling change upon filing its supplemental application with the FDA; it need not wait for FDA approval.

Wyeth argues that the CBE regulation is not implicated in this case because a 2008 amendment provides that a manufacturer may only change its label "to reflect newly acquired information." Resting on this language (which Wyeth argues simply reaffirmed the interpretation of the regulation in effect when this case was tried), Wyeth contends that it could have changed Phenergan's label only in response to new information that the FDA had not considered. And it maintains that Levine has not pointed to any such information concerning the risks of IV-push administration. Thus, Wyeth insists, it was impossible for it to discharge its state-law obligation to provide a stronger warning about IV-push administration without violating federal law. Wyeth's argument misapprehends both the federal drug regulatory scheme and its burden in establishing a pre-emption defense.

Wyeth could have revised Phenergan's label even in accordance with the amended regulation. As the FDA explained in its notice of the final rule, "newly acquired information" is not limited to new data, but also encompasses "new analyses of previously submitted data." The rule accounts for the fact that risk information accumulates over time and that the same data may take on a different meaning in light of subsequent developments.

Wyeth argues that if it had unilaterally added such a warning, it would have violated federal law governing unauthorized distribution and misbranding. Its argument that a change in Phenergan's labeling would have subjected it to liability for unauthorized distribution rests on the assumption that this labeling change would have rendered Phenergan a new drug lacking an effective application. But strengthening the warning about IV-push administration would not have made Phenergan a new drug. Nor would this warning have rendered Phenergan misbranded. The FDCA does not provide that a drug is misbranded simply because the manufacturer has altered an FDA-approved label; instead, the misbranding provision focuses on the substance of the label and, among other things, proscribes labels that fail to include "adequate warnings."

Of course, the FDA retains authority to reject labeling changes made pursuant to the CBE regulation in its review of the manufacturer's supplemental application, just as it retains such authority in reviewing all supplemental applications. But absent clear evidence that the FDA would not have approved a change to Phenergan's label, we will not conclude that it was impossible for Wyeth to comply with both federal and state requirements. Wyeth has offered no such evidence.

Impossibility pre-emption is a demanding defense. On the record before us, Wyeth has failed to demonstrate that it was impossible for it to comply with both federal and state requirements. The CBE regulation permitted Wyeth to unilaterally strengthen its warning, and the mere fact that the FDA approved Phenergan's label does not establish that it would have prohibited such a change.

IV

Wyeth also argues that requiring it to comply with a state-law duty to provide a stronger warning about IV-push administration would obstruct the purposes and objectives of federal drug labeling regulation. Levine's tort claims, it maintains, are pre-empted because they interfere with "Congress's purpose to entrust an expert agency to make drug labeling decisions that strike a balance between competing objectives." We find no merit in this argument, which relies on an untenable interpretation of congressional intent and an overbroad view of an agency's power to pre-empt state law.

Wyeth contends that the FDCA establishes both a floor and a ceiling for drug regulation: Once the FDA has approved a drug's label, a state-law verdict may not deem the label inadequate, regardless of whether there is any evidence that the FDA has considered the stronger warning at issue. The most glaring problem with this argument is that all evidence of Congress' purposes is to the contrary. Building on its 1906 Act, Congress enacted the FDCA to bolster consumer protection against harmful products. Congress did not provide a federal remedy for consumers harmed by unsafe or ineffective drugs in the 1938 statute or in any subsequent amendment. Evidently, it determined that widely available state rights of action provided appropriate relief for injured consumers. It may also have recognized that state-law remedies further consumer protection by motivating manufacturers to produce safe and effective drugs and to give adequate warnings.

If Congress thought state-law suits posed an obstacle to its objectives, it surely would have enacted an express pre-emption provision at some point during the FDCA's 70-year history. But despite its 1976 enactment of an express pre-emption provision for medical devices, Congress has not enacted such a provision for prescription drugs. Its silence on the issue, coupled with its certain awareness of the prevalence of state tort litigation, is powerful evidence that Congress did not intend FDA oversight to be the exclusive means of ensuring drug safety and effectiveness.

In keeping with Congress' decision not to pre-empt common-law tort suits, it appears that the FDA traditionally regarded state law as a complementary form of drug regulation. The FDA has limited resources to monitor the 11,000 drugs on the market, and manufacturers have superior access to information about their drugs, especially in the post-marketing phase as new risks emerge. State tort suits uncover unknown drug hazards and provide incentives for drug manufacturers to disclose safety risks promptly. They also serve a distinct compensatory function that may motivate injured persons to come forward with information. Failure-to-warn actions, in particular, lend force to the FDCA's premise that manufacturers, not the FDA, bear primary responsibility for their drug labeling at all times. Thus, the FDA long maintained that state law offers an additional, and important, layer of consumer protection that complements FDA regulation.

V

We conclude that it is not impossible for Wyeth to comply with its state and federal law obligations and that Levine's common-law claims do not stand as an obstacle to the accomplishment of Congress' purposes in the FDCA.

Justice THOMAS, concurring in the judgment.

I agree with the Court that the fact that the Food and Drug Administration (FDA) approved the label for petitioner Wyeth's drug Phenergan does not pre-empt the state-law judgment before the Court. I write separately, however, because I cannot join the majority's implicit endorsement of far-reaching implied pre-emption doctrines. In particular, I have become increasingly skeptical of this Court's "purposes and objectives" pre-emption jurisprudence. Under this approach, the Court routinely invalidates state laws based on perceived conflicts with broad federal policy objectives, legislative history, or generalized notions of congressional purposes that are not embodied within the text of federal law. Because implied pre-emption doctrines that wander far from the statutory text are inconsistent with the Constitution, I concur only in the judgment.

In order "to ensure the protection of our fundamental liberties," the "Constitution establishes a system of dual sovereignty between the States and the Federal Government." The Framers adopted this "constitutionally mandated balance of power," to "reduce the risk of tyranny and abuse from either front," because a "federalist structure of joint sovereigns preserves to the people numerous advantages," such as "a decentralized government that will be more sensitive to the diverse needs of a heterogeneous society" and "increase[d] opportunity for citizen involvement in democratic processes." Furthermore, as the Framers observed, the "compound republic of America" provides "a double security . . . to the rights of the people" because "the power surrendered by the people is first divided between two distinct governments, and then the portion allotted to each subdivided among distinct and separate departments." The Federalist No. 51, p. 266 (M. Beloff ed., 2d ed.1987).

Under this federalist system, "the States possess sovereignty concurrent with that of the Federal Government, subject only to limitations imposed by the Supremacy Clause." In this way, the Supremacy Clause gives the Federal Government "a decided advantage in [a] delicate balance" between federal and state sovereigns. "As long as it is acting within the powers granted it under the Constitution, Congress may impose its will on the States." That is an "extraordinary power in a federalist system."

In light of these constitutional principles, I have become "increasing[ly] reluctan[t] to expand federal statutes beyond their terms through doctrines of implied pre-emption." My review of this Court's broad implied pre-emption precedents, particularly its "purposes and objectives" pre-emption jurisprudence, has increased my concerns that implied pre-emption doctrines have not always been constitutionally applied. Under the vague and "potentially boundless" doctrine of "purposes and objectives" pre-emption, in [this case], the relevant federal law did not give Wyeth a right that the state-law judgment took away, and it was possible for Wyeth to comply with both federal law and the Vermont-law judgment at issue here. The federal statute and regulations neither prohibited the stronger warning label required by the state judgment, nor insulated Wyeth from the risk of state-law liability. With no "direct conflict" between the federal and state law, then, the state-law judgment is not pre-empted.

The origins of this Court's "purposes and objectives" pre-emption jurisprudence and its broad application illustrate that this brand of the Court's pre-emption jurisprudence facilitates freewheeling, extratextual, and broad evaluations of the "purposes and objectives" embodied within federal law. This, in turn, leads to decisions giving improperly broad pre-emptive effect to judicially manufactured policies, rather than to the statutory text enacted by Congress pursuant to the Constitution and the agency actions authorized thereby. Because such a sweeping approach to pre-emption leads to the illegitimate—and thus, unconstitutional—invalidation of state laws, I can no longer assent to a doctrine that pre-empts state laws merely because they "stan[d] as an obstacle to the accomplishment and execution of the full purposes and objectives" of federal law, as perceived by this Court.

Justice ALITO, with whom the CHIEF JUSTICE and Justice SCALIA join, dissenting.

This case illustrates that tragic facts make bad law. The Court holds that a state tort jury, rather than the Food and Drug Administration (FDA), is ultimately responsible for regulating warning labels for prescription drugs. That result cannot be reconciled with or general principles of conflict pre-emption. I respectfully dissent.

I

The Court frames the question presented as a "narro[w]" one—namely, whether Wyeth has a duty to provide "an adequate warning about using the IV-push method" to administer Phenergan. But that ignores the antecedent question of who—the FDA or a jury in Vermont—has the authority and responsibility for determining the "adequacy" of Phenergan's warnings. Moreover, it is unclear how a "stronger" warning could have helped respondent, after all, the physician's assistant who treated her disregarded at least six separate warnings that are already on Phenergan's labeling, so respondent would be hard pressed to prove that a seventh would have made a difference.

More to the point, the question presented by this case is not a "narrow" one, and it does not concern whether Phenergan's label should bear a "stronger" warning. Rather, the real issue is whether a state tort jury can countermand the FDA's considered judgment that Phenergan's FDA-mandated warning label renders its intravenous (IV) use "safe." Indeed, respondent's amended complaint alleged that Phenergan is "not reasonably safe for intravenous administration." [R]espondent's attorney told the jury that Phenergan's label should say, "Do not use this drug intravenously," respondent's expert told the jury, "I think the drug should be labeled 'Not for IV use," and during his closing argument, respondent's attorney told the jury, "Thank God we don't rely on the FDA to . . . make the safe[ty] decision. You will make the decision. . . . The FDA doesn't make the decision, you do." Federal law, however, *does* rely on the FDA to make safety determinations like the one it made here. The FDA has long known about the risks associated with IV push in general and its use to administer Phenergan in particular. Whether wisely or not, the FDA has concluded—over the course of extensive, 54-year-long regulatory proceedings—that the drug is "safe" and "effective" when used in accordance with its FDA-mandated labeling. The unfortunate fact that respondent's healthcare providers ignored Phenergan's labeling may make this an ideal medical-malpractice case. But turning a common-law tort suit into a "frontal assault" on the FDA's regulatory regime for drug labeling upsets the well-settled meaning of the Supremacy Clause and our conflict pre-emption jurisprudence.

II

To the extent that "[t]he purpose of Congress is the ultimate touchstone in every pre-emption case," Congress made its "purpose" plain in authorizing the FDA—not state tort juries—to determine when and under what circumstances a drug is "safe." Where the FDA determines, in accordance with its statutory mandate, that a drug is on balance "safe," our conflict pre-emption cases prohibit any State from countermanding that determination.

A faithful application of this Court's conflict pre-emption cases compels the conclusion that the FDA's 40-year-long effort to regulate the safety and efficacy of Phenergan pre-empts respondent's tort suit.

Phenergan's warning label has been subject to the FDA's strict regulatory oversight since the 1950's. For at least the last 34 years, the FDA has focused specifically on whether IV-push administration of Phenergan is "safe" and "effective" when performed in accordance with Phenergan's label. The agency's ultimate decision—to retain IV push as one means for administering Phenergan, albeit subject to stringent warnings—is reflected in the plain text of Phenergan's label (sometimes in boldfaced font and all-capital letters). And the record contains ample evidence that the FDA specifically considered and reconsidered the strength of Phenergan's IV-push-related warnings in light of new scientific and medical data. The majority's factual assertions to the contrary are mistaken.

By their very nature, juries are ill-equipped to perform the FDA's cost-benefit-balancing function. [J]uries tend to focus on the risk of a particular product's design or warning label that arguably contributed to a particular plaintiff's injury, not on the overall benefits of that design or label; "the patients who reaped those benefits are not represented in court." Indeed, patients like respondent are the only ones whom tort juries ever see, and for a patient like respondent-who has already suffered a tragic accident—Phenergan's risks are no longer a matter of probabilities and potentialities.

In contrast, the FDA has the benefit of the long view. Its drug-approval determinations consider the interests of all potential users of a drug, including "those who would suffer without new medical [products]" if juries in all 50 States were free to contradict the FDA's expert determinations. And the FDA conveys its warnings with one voice, rather than whipsawing the medical community with 50 (or more) potentially conflicting ones. After today's ruling, however, parochialism may prevail.

To be sure, state tort suits can peacefully coexist with the FDA's labeling regime, and they have done so for decades. But this case is far from peaceful coexistence. The FDA told Wyeth that Phenergan's label renders its use "safe." But the State of Vermont, through its tort law, said: "Not so."

Chapter 5

The Structure of the Constitution's Protection of Individual Liberties

B. The Application of the Bill of Rights to the States (casebook, p. 523)

3. The incorporation of the Bill of Rights into the Due Process Clause of the Fourteenth Amendment (casebook, p. 536)

In *District of Columbia v. Heller* (2008) (casebook, p. 13), the Supreme Court held that the Second Amendment is not limited to protecting a right to have firearms for militia service; it protects an individual's right to have guns, at least for self-protection in the home. Because the District of Columbia is a part of the federal government, the Court had no occasion to consider whether the Second Amendment applies to state and local governments. In *McDonald v. City of Chicago* (2010), the Court addressed this and held 5-4 that the Second Amendment applies to state and local governments. Justice Alito, writing for a plurality of four, used incorporation into the due process clause to accomplish this. Justice Thomas, concurring and concurring in the judgment, would have used the privileges or immunities clause of the Fourteenth Amendment.

McDONALD v. CITY OF CHICAGO
130 S.Ct. _____ (2010)

Justice ALITO announced the judgment of the Court

Two years ago, in *District of Columbia v. Heller* (2008), we held that the Second Amendment protects the right to keep and bear arms for the purpose of self-defense, and we struck down a District of Columbia law that banned the possession of handguns in the home. The city of Chicago (City) and the village of Oak Park, a Chicago suburb, have laws that are similar to the District of Columbia's, but Chicago and Oak Park argue that their laws are constitutional because the Second Amendment has no application to the States. We have previously held that most of the provisions of the Bill of Rights apply with full force to both the Federal Government and the States. Applying the standard that is well established in our case law, we hold that the Second Amendment right is fully applicable to the States.

I

Otis McDonald, Adam Orlov, Colleen Lawson, and David Lawson (Chicago petitioners) are Chicago residents who would like to keep handguns in their homes for self-defense but are prohibited from doing so by Chicago's firearms laws. A City ordinance provides that "[n]o person shall . . . possess . . . any firearm unless such person is the holder of a valid registration certificate for such firearm." The Code then prohibits registration of most handguns, thus effectively banning handgun possession by almost all private citizens who reside in the City. Like Chicago, Oak Park makes it "unlawful for any person to possess . . . any firearm," a term that includes "pistols, revolvers, guns and small arms . . . commonly known as handguns."

Chicago enacted its handgun ban to protect its residents "from the loss of property and injury or death from firearms." The Chicago petitioners and their *amici,* however, argue that the handgun ban has left them vulnerable to criminals. Chicago Police Department statistics, we are told, reveal that the City's handgun murder rate has actually increased since the ban was enacted and that Chicago residents now face one of the highest murder rates in the country and rates of other violent crimes that exceed the average in comparable cities.

II

Petitioners argue that the Chicago and Oak Park laws violate the right to keep and bear arms for two reasons. Petitioners' primary submission is that this right is among the "privileges or immunities of citizens of the United States" and that the narrow interpretation of the Privileges or Immunities Clause adopted in the *Slaughter-House Cases* (1873), should now be rejected. As a secondary argument, petitioners contend that the Fourteenth Amendment's Due Process Clause "incorporates" the Second Amendment right.

Chicago and Oak Park (municipal respondents) maintain that a right set out in the Bill of Rights applies to the States only if that right is an indispensable attribute of *any* "'civilized'" legal system. If it is possible to imagine a civilized country that does not recognize the right, the municipal respondents tell us, then that right is not protected by due process. And since there are civilized countries that ban or strictly regulate the private possession of handguns, the municipal respondents maintain that due process does not preclude such measures.

Petitioners argue, however, that we should overrule [earlier] decisions and hold that the right to keep and bear arms is one of the "privileges or immunities of citizens of the United States." In petitioners' view, the Privileges or Immunities Clause protects all of the rights set out in the Bill of Rights, as well as some others, but petitioners are unable to identify the Clause's full scope. Nor is there any consensus on that question among the scholars who agree that the *Slaughter-House Cases'* interpretation is flawed.

We see no need to reconsider that interpretation here. For many decades, the question of the rights protected by the Fourteenth Amendment against state infringement has been analyzed under the Due Process Clause of that Amendment and not under the Privileges or Immunities Clause. We therefore decline to disturb the *Slaughter-House* holding.

[The Court then reviewed the history of incorporation in detail.]

III

With this framework in mind, we now turn directly to the question whether the Second Amendment right to keep and bear arms is incorporated in the concept of due process. In answering that question, as just explained, we must decide whether the right to keep and bear arms is fundamental to *our* scheme of ordered liberty, or as we have said in a related context, whether this right is "deeply rooted in this Nation's history and tradition."

Our decision in *Heller* points unmistakably to the answer. Self-defense is a basic right, recognized by many legal systems from ancient times to the present day, and in *Heller,* we held that individual self-defense is "the *central component*" of the Second Amendment right. Explaining that "the need for defense of self, family, and property is most acute" in the home, we found that this right applies to handguns because they are "the most preferred firearm in the nation to 'keep' and use for protection of one's home and family." Thus, we concluded, citizens must be permitted "to use [handguns] for the core lawful purpose of self-defense."

Heller makes it clear that this right is "deeply rooted in this Nation's history and tradition." *Heller* explored the right's origins, noting that the

1689 English Bill of Rights explicitly protected a right to keep arms for self-defense, and that by 1765, Blackstone was able to assert that the right to keep and bear arms was "one of the fundamental rights of Englishmen." Blackstone's assessment was shared by the American colonists. As we noted in *Heller,* King George III's attempt to disarm the colonists in the 1760's and 1770's "provoked polemical reactions by Americans invoking their rights as Englishmen to keep arms."

The right to keep and bear arms was considered no less fundamental by those who drafted and ratified the Bill of Rights. "During the 1788 ratification debates, the fear that the federal government would disarm the people in order to impose rule through a standing army or select militia was pervasive in Antifederalist rhetoric." Federalists responded, not by arguing that the right was insufficiently important to warrant protection but by contending that the right was adequately protected by the Constitution's assignment of only limited powers to the Federal Government. Thus, Antifederalists and Federalists alike agreed that the right to bear arms was fundamental to the newly formed system of government.

This understanding persisted in the years immediately following the ratification of the Bill of Rights. In addition to the four States that had adopted Second Amendment analogues before ratification, nine more States adopted state constitutional provisions protecting an individual right to keep and bear arms between 1789 and 1820.

By the 1850's, the perceived threat that had prompted the inclusion of the Second Amendment in the Bill of Rights—the fear that the National Government would disarm the universal militia—had largely faded as a popular concern, but the right to keep and bear arms was highly valued for purposes of self-defense. Abolitionist authors wrote in support of the right. And when attempts were made to disarm "Free-Soilers" in "Bloody Kansas," Senator Charles Sumner, who later played a leading role in the adoption of the Fourteenth Amendment, proclaimed that "[n]ever was [the rifle] more needed in just self-defense than now in Kansas."

After the Civil War, many of the over 180,000 African Americans who served in the Union Army returned to the States of the old Confederacy, where systematic efforts were made to disarm them and other blacks. The laws of some States formally prohibited African Americans from possessing firearms. Union Army commanders took steps to secure the right of all citizens to keep and bear arms, but the 39th Congress concluded that legislative action was necessary. Its efforts to safeguard the right to keep and bear arms demonstrate that the right was still recognized to be fundamental. The Civil Rights Act of 1866, which was considered at the same time as the Freedmen's Bureau Act, sought to protect the right of all citizens to keep and bear arms.

In debating the Fourteenth Amendment, the 39th Congress referred to the right to keep and bear arms as a fundamental right deserving of protection. Senator Samuel Pomeroy described three "indispensable" "safeguards of liberty under our form of Government." One of these, he said, was the right to keep and bear arms. Even those who thought the Fourteenth Amendment unnecessary believed that blacks, as citizens, "have equal right to protection, and to keep and bear arms for self-defense."

Evidence from the period immediately following the ratification of the Fourteenth Amendment only confirms that the right to keep and bear arms was considered fundamental. The right to keep and bear arms was also widely protected by state constitutions at the time when the Fourteenth Amendment was ratified. In 1868, 22 of the 37 States in the Union had state constitutional provisions explicitly protecting the right to keep and bear arms.

In sum, it is clear that the Framers and ratifiers of the Fourteenth Amendment counted the right to keep and bear arms among those fundamental rights necessary to our system of ordered liberty.

IV

Municipal respondents' remaining arguments are at war with our central holding in *Heller*: that the Second Amendment protects a personal right to keep and bear arms for lawful purposes, most notably for self-defense within the home. Municipal respondents, in effect, ask us to treat the right recognized in *Heller* as a second-class right, subject to an entirely different body of rules than the other Bill of Rights guarantees that we have held to be incorporated into the Due Process Clause.

Municipal respondents' main argument is nothing less than a plea to disregard 50 years of incorporation precedent and return (presumably for this case only) to a bygone era. Municipal respondents submit that the Due Process Clause protects only those rights "'recognized by all temperate and civilized governments, from a deep and universal sense of [their] justice.'" According to municipal respondents, if it is possible to imagine *any* civilized legal system that does not recognize a particular right, then the Due Process Clause does not make that right binding on the States. Therefore, the municipal respondents continue, because such countries as England, Canada, Australia, Japan, Denmark, Finland, Luxembourg, and New Zealand either ban or severely limit handgun ownership, it must follow that no right to possess such weapons is protected by the Fourteenth Amendment.

This line of argument is, of course, inconsistent with the long-established standard we apply in incorporation cases. And the present-day implications of municipal respondents' argument are stunning. For example, many of the rights that our Bill of Rights provides for persons accused of criminal offenses are virtually unique to this country. If *our* understanding of the right to a jury trial, the right against self-incrimination, and the right to counsel were necessary attributes of *any* civilized country, it would follow that the United States is the only civilized Nation in the world.

Municipal respondents maintain that the Second Amendment differs from all of the other provisions of the Bill of Rights because it concerns the right to possess a deadly implement and thus has implications for public safety. And they note that there is intense disagreement on the question whether the private possession of guns in the home increases or decreases gun deaths and injuries.

The right to keep and bear arms, however, is not the only constitutional right that has controversial public safety implications. All of the constitutional provisions that impose restrictions on law enforcement and on the prosecution of crimes fall into the same category.

It is important to keep in mind that *Heller,* while striking down a law that prohibited the possession of handguns in the home, recognized that the right to keep and bear arms is not "a right to keep and carry any weapon whatsoever in any manner whatsoever and for whatever purpose." We made it clear in *Heller* that our holding did not cast doubt on such longstanding regulatory measures as "prohibitions on the possession of firearms by felons and the mentally ill," "laws forbidding the carrying of firearms in sensitive places such as schools and government buildings, or laws imposing conditions and qualifications on the commercial sale of arms." We repeat those assurances here. Despite municipal respondents' doomsday proclamations, incorporation does not imperil every law regulating firearms.

* * *

In *Heller,* we held that the Second Amendment protects the right to possess a handgun in the home for the purpose of self-defense. Unless considerations of *stare decisis* counsel otherwise, a provision of the Bill of Rights that protects a right that is fundamental from an American perspective applies equally to the Federal Government and the States. We therefore hold that the Due Process Clause of the Fourteenth Amendment incorporates the Second Amendment right recognized in *Heller.*

The judgment of the Court of Appeals is reversed, and the case is remanded for further proceedings.

Justice SCALIA, concurring.

I join the Court's opinion. Despite my misgivings about Substantive Due Process as an original matter, I have acquiesced in the Court's incorporation of certain guarantees in the Bill of Rights "because it is both long established and narrowly limited." This case does not require me to reconsider that view, since straightforward application of settled doctrine suffices to decide it.

[Justice SCALIA then engaged in a lengthy response to Justice STEVENS' dissent, which defended constitutional interpretation based on a "living Constitution." He concluded his dissent by saying:] And the Court's approach intrudes less upon the democratic process because the rights it acknowledges are those established by a constitutional history formed by democratic decisions; and the rights it fails to acknowledge are left to be democratically adopted or rejected by the people, with the assurance that their decision is not subject to judicial revision. Justice Stevens' approach, on the other hand, deprives the people of that power, since whatever the Constitution and laws may say, the list of protected rights will be whatever courts wish it to be. After all, he notes, the people have been wrong before, and courts may conclude they are wrong in the future. Justice Stevens abhors a system in which "majorities or powerful interest groups always get their way," but replaces it with a system in which unelected and life-tenured judges always get their way. That such usurpation is effected unabashedly, with "the judge's cards . . . laid on the table," *ibid.*—makes it even worse. In a vibrant democracy, usurpation should have to be accomplished in the dark. It is Justice Stevens' approach, not the Court's, that puts democracy in peril.

Justice THOMAS, concurring in part and concurring in the judgment.

I agree with the Court that the Fourteenth Amendment makes the right to keep and bear arms set forth in the Second Amendment "fully applicable to the States." I write separately because I believe there is a more straightforward path to this conclusion, one that is more faithful to the Fourteenth Amendment's text and history.

I

Applying what is now a well-settled test, the plurality opinion concludes that the right to keep and bear arms applies to the States through the Fourteenth Amendment's Due Process Clause because it is "fundamental" to the American "scheme of ordered liberty," and "'deeply rooted in this Nation's history and tradition.'" I agree with that description of the right. But I cannot agree that it is enforceable against the States through a clause that speaks only to "process." Instead, the right to keep and bear arms is a privilege of American citizenship that applies to the States through the Fourteenth Amendment's Privileges or Immunities Clause.

The meaning of § 1's next sentence has divided this Court for many years. That sentence begins with the command that "[n]o State shall make or enforce any law which shall abridge the privileges or immunities of citizens of the United States." On its face, this appears to grant the persons just made United States citizens a certain collection of rights—*i.e.,* privileges or immunities—attributable to that status.

This Court's precedents accept that point, but define the relevant collection of rights quite narrowly. In the *Slaughter-House Cases* (1873), decided just five years after the Fourteenth Amendment's adoption, the Court interpreted this text, now known as the Privileges or Immunities Clause, for the first time. As a consequence of this Court's marginalization of the Clause, litigants seeking federal protection of fundamental rights turned to the remainder of § 1 in search of an alternative fount of such rights. They found one in a most curious place—that section's command that every State guarantee "due process" to any person before depriving him of "life, liberty, or property." At first, litigants argued that this Due Process Clause "incorporated" certain procedural rights codified in the Bill of Rights against the States. The Court generally rejected those claims, however, on the theory that the rights in question were not sufficiently "fundamental" to warrant such treatment.

That changed with time. The Court came to conclude that certain Bill of Rights guarantees *were* sufficiently fundamental to fall within § 1's guarantee of "due process." These included not only procedural protections listed in the first eight Amendments, but substantive rights as well.

All of this is a legal fiction. The notion that a constitutional provision that guarantees only "process" before a person is deprived of life, liberty, or property could define the substance of those rights strains credulity for even the most casual user of words. Moreover, this fiction is a particularly dangerous one. The one theme that links the Court's substantive due process precedents together is their lack of a guiding principle to distinguish "fundamental" rights that warrant protection from nonfundamental rights that do not. Today's decision illustrates the point.

To be sure, the plurality's effort to cabin the exercise of judicial discretion under the Due Process Clause by focusing its inquiry on those rights deeply rooted in American history and tradition invites less opportunity for abuse than the alternatives. But any serious argument over the scope of the Due Process Clause must acknowledge that neither its text nor its history suggests that it protects the many substantive rights this Court's cases now claim it does.

I cannot accept a theory of constitutional interpretation that rests on such tenuous footing. This Court's substantive due process framework fails to account for both the text of the Fourteenth Amendment and the history that led to its adoption, filling that gap with a jurisprudence devoid of a guiding principle. I believe the original meaning of the Fourteenth Amendment offers a superior alternative, and that a return to that meaning would allow this Court to enforce the rights the Fourteenth Amendment is designed to protect with greater clarity and predictability than the substantive due process framework has so far managed.

I acknowledge the volume of precedents that have been built upon the substantive due process framework, and I further acknowledge the importance of *stare decisis* to the stability of our Nation's legal system. But *stare decisis* is only an "adjunct" of our duty as judges to decide by our best lights what the Constitution means. Moreover, as judges, we interpret the Constitution one case or controversy at a time. The question presented in this case is not whether our entire Fourteenth Amendment jurisprudence must be preserved or revised, but only whether, and to what extent, a particular clause in the Constitution protects the particular right at issue here. With the inquiry appropriately narrowed, I believe this case presents an opportunity to reexamine, and begin the process of restoring, the meaning of the Fourteenth Amendment agreed upon by those who ratified it.

II

"It cannot be presumed that any clause in the constitution is intended to be without effect." Because the Court's Privileges or Immunities Clause precedents have presumed just that, I set them aside for the moment and begin with the text.

The Privileges or Immunities Clause of the Fourteenth Amendment declares that "[n]o State . . . shall abridge the privileges or immunities of citizens of the United States." At the time of Reconstruction, the terms "privileges" and "immunities" had an established meaning as synonyms for "rights." The two words, standing alone or paired together, were used interchangeably with the words "rights," "liberties," and "freedoms," and had been since the time of Blackstone. The group of rights-bearers to whom the Privileges or Immunities Clause applies is, of course, "citizens." By the time of Reconstruction, it had long been established that both the States and the Federal Government existed to preserve their citizens' inalienable rights, and that these rights were considered "privileges" or "immunities" of citizenship.

The text examined so far demonstrates three points about the meaning of the Privileges or Immunities Clause in § 1. First, "privileges" and "immunities" were synonyms for "rights." Second, both the States and the Federal Government had long recognized the inalienable rights of their citizens. Third, Article IV, § 2 of the Constitution protected traveling citizens against state discrimination with respect to the fundamental rights of state citizenship.

[Justice THOMAS then argued that stare decisis should not preclude this use of the privileges or immunities clause.]

* * *

I agree with the Court that the Second Amendment is fully applicable to the States. I do so because the right to keep and bear arms is guaranteed by the Fourteenth Amendment as a privilege of American citizenship.

Justice STEVENS, dissenting.

In *District of Columbia v. Heller* (2008), the Court answered the question whether a federal enclave's "prohibition on the possession of usable handguns in the home violates the Second Amendment to the Constitution." The question we should be answering in this case is whether the Constitution "guarantees individuals a fundamental right," enforceable against the States, "to possess a functional, personal firearm, including a handgun, within the home." That is a different—and more difficult—inquiry than asking if the Fourteenth Amendment "incorporates" the Second Amendment. The so-called incorporation question was squarely and, in my view, correctly resolved in the late 19th century.

I agree with the plurality's refusal to accept petitioners' primary submission. Their briefs marshal an impressive amount of historical evidence for their argument that the Court interpreted the Privileges or Immunities Clause too narrowly in the *Slaughter-House Cases* (1873). But the original meaning of the Clause is not as clear as they suggest—and not nearly as clear as it would need to be to dislodge 137 years of precedent. The burden is severe for those who seek radical change in such an established body of constitutional doctrine. Moreover, the suggestion that invigorating the Privileges or Immunities Clause will reduce judicial discretion, strikes me as implausible, if not exactly backwards. "For the very reason that it has so long remained a clean slate, a revitalized Privileges or Immunities Clause holds special hazards for judges who are mindful that their proper task is not to write their personal views of appropriate public policy into the Constitution."

I further agree with the plurality that there are weighty arguments supporting petitioners' second submission, insofar as it concerns the possession of firearms for lawful self-defense in the home. But these arguments are less compelling than the plurality suggests; they are much less compelling when applied outside the home; and their validity does not depend on the Court's holding in *Heller*. For that holding sheds no light on the meaning of the Due Process Clause of the Fourteenth Amendment. Our decisions construing that Clause to render various procedural guarantees in the Bill of Rights enforceable against the States likewise tell us little about the meaning of the word "liberty" in the Clause or about the scope of its protection of nonprocedural rights.

This is a substantive due process case. [Justice STEVENS then reviewed the history of substantive due process and explained his view that the meaning of due process evolves and that it is not limited to the original understanding.]

[III]

The question in this case, then, is not whether the Second Amendment right to keep and bear arms (whatever that right's precise contours) applies to the States because the Amendment has been incorporated into the Fourteenth Amendment. It has not been. The question, rather, is whether the particular right asserted by petitioners applies to the States because of the Fourteenth Amendment itself, standing on its own bottom. And to answer that question, we need to determine, first, the nature of the right that has been asserted and, second, whether that right is an aspect of Fourteenth Amendment "liberty." Even accepting the Court's holding in *Heller,* it remains entirely possible that the right to keep and bear arms identified in that opinion is not judicially enforceable against the States, or that only part of the right is so enforceable. It is likewise possible for the Court to find in this case that some part of the *Heller* right applies to the States, and then to find in later cases that other parts of the right also apply, or apply on different terms.

While I agree with the Court that our substantive due process cases offer a principled basis for holding that petitioners have a constitutional right to possess a usable firearm in the home, I am ultimately persuaded that a better reading of our case law supports the city of Chicago. I would not foreclose the possibility that a particular plaintiff—say, an elderly widow who lives in a dangerous neighborhood and does not have the strength to operate a long gun—may have a cognizable liberty interest in possessing a handgun. But I cannot accept petitioners' broader submission. A number of factors, taken together, lead me to this conclusion.

First, firearms have a fundamentally ambivalent relationship to liberty. Just as they can help homeowners defend their families and property from intruders, they can help thugs and insurrectionists murder innocent victims. The threat that firearms will be misused is far from hypothetical, for gun crime has devastated many of our communities. *Amici* calculate that approximately one million Americans have been wounded or killed by gunfire in the last decade. Urban areas such as Chicago suffer disproportionately from this epidemic of violence. Handguns contribute disproportionately to it. Just as some homeowners may prefer handguns because of their small size, light weight, and ease of operation, some criminals will value them for the same reasons. In recent years, handguns were reportedly used in more than four-fifths of firearm murders and more than half of all murders nationwide.

Hence, in evaluating an asserted right to be free from particular gun-control regulations, liberty is on both sides of the equation. Guns may be useful for self-defense, as well as for hunting and sport, but they also have a unique potential to facilitate death and destruction and thereby to destabilize ordered liberty. *Your* interest in keeping and bearing a certain firearm may diminish *my* interest in being and feeling safe from armed violence. And while granting you the right to own a handgun might make you safer on any given day—assuming the handgun's marginal contribution to self-defense outweighs its marginal contribution to the risk of accident, suicide, and criminal mischief—it may make you and the community you live in less safe overall, owing to the increased number of handguns in circulation. It is at least reasonable for a democratically elected legislature to take such concerns into account in considering what sorts of regulations would best serve the public welfare.

The practical impact of various gun-control measures may be highly controversial, but this basic insight should not be. The idea that deadly weapons pose a distinctive threat to the social order—and that reasonable restrictions on their usage therefore impose an acceptable burden on one's personal liberty—is as old as the Republic.

Limiting the federal constitutional right to keep and bear arms to the home complicates the analysis but does not dislodge this conclusion. Even though the Court has long afforded special solicitude for the privacy of the home, we have never understood that principle to "infring[e] upon" the authority of the States to proscribe certain inherently dangerous items, for "[i]n such cases, compelling reasons may exist for overriding the right of the individual to possess those materials." And, of course, guns that start out in the home may not stay in the home. Even if the government has a weaker basis for restricting domestic possession of firearms as compared to public carriage—and even if a blanket, statewide prohibition on domestic possession might therefore be unconstitutional—the line between the two is a porous one. A state or local legislature may determine that a prophylactic ban on an especially portable weapon is necessary to police that line.

Second, the right to possess a firearm of one's choosing is different in kind from the liberty interests we have recognized under the Due Process Clause. Despite the plethora of substantive due process cases that have been decided in the post-*Lochner* century, I have found none that holds, states, or even suggests that the term "liberty" encompasses either the common-law right of self-defense or a right to keep and bear arms. I do not doubt for a moment that many Americans feel deeply passionate about firearms, and see them as critical to their way of life as well as to their security. Nevertheless, it does not appear to be the case that the ability to own a handgun, or any particular type of firearm, is critical to leading a life of autonomy, dignity, or political equality: The marketplace offers many tools for self-defense, even if they are imperfect substitutes, and neither petitioners nor their *amici* make such a contention.

Third, the experience of other advanced democracies, including those that share our British heritage, undercuts the notion that an expansive right to keep and bear arms is intrinsic to ordered liberty. Many of these countries place restrictions on the possession, use, and carriage of firearms far more onerous than the restrictions found in this Nation. That the United States is an international outlier in the permissiveness of its approach to guns does not suggest that our laws are bad laws. It does suggest that this Court may not need to assume responsibility for making our laws still more permissive.

Admittedly, these other countries differ from ours in many relevant respects, including their problems with violent crime and the traditional role that firearms have played in their societies. But they are not so different from the United States that we ought to dismiss their experience entirely. The fact that our oldest allies have almost uniformly found it appropriate to regulate firearms extensively tends to weaken petitioners' submission that the right to possess a gun of one's choosing is fundamental to a life of liberty. While the "American perspective" must always be our focus, it is silly—indeed, arrogant—to think we have nothing to learn about liberty from the billions of people beyond our borders.

Nor will the Court's intervention bring any clarity to this enormously complex area of law. Quite to the contrary, today's decision invites an avalanche of litigation that could mire the federal courts in fine-grained determinations about which state and local regulations comport with the *Heller* right-the precise contours of which are far from pellucid—under a standard of review we have not even established. The plurality's "assuranc [e]" that "incorporation does not imperil every law regulating firearms," provides only modest comfort. For it is also an admission of just how many different types of regulations are potentially implicated by today's ruling, and of just how ad hoc the Court's initial attempt to draw distinctions among them was in *Heller*. The practical significance of the proposition that "the Second Amendment right is fully applicable to the States," remains to be worked out by this Court over many, many years.

Furthermore, and critically, the Court's imposition of a national standard is still more unwise because the elected branches have shown themselves to be perfectly capable of safeguarding the interest in keeping and bearing arms. The strength of a liberty claim must be assessed in connection with its status in the democratic process. And in this case, no one disputes "that opponents of [gun] control have considerable political power and do not seem to be at a systematic disadvantage in the democratic process," or that "the widespread commitment to an individual right to own guns . . . operates as a safeguard against excessive or unjustified gun control laws." Indeed, there is a good deal of evidence to suggest that, if anything, American lawmakers tend to *under* regulate guns, relative to the policy views expressed by majorities in opinion polls. If a particular State or locality has enacted some "improvident" gun-control measures, as petitioners believe Chicago has done, there is no apparent reason to infer that the mistake will not "eventually be rectified by the democratic process."

I would proceed more cautiously. For the reasons set out at length above, I cannot accept either the methodology the Court employs or the conclusions it draws. Although impressively argued, the majority's decision to overturn more than a century of Supreme Court precedent and to unsettle a much longer tradition of state practice is not, in my judg-ment, built "upon respect for the teachings of history, solid recognition of the basic values that underlie our society, and wise appreciation of the great roles that the doctrines of federalism and separation of powers have played in establishing and preserving American freedoms."

Justice BREYER, with whom Justice GINSBURG and Justice SOTOMAYOR join, dissenting.

I can find nothing in the Second Amendment's text, history, or under-lying rationale that could warrant characterizing it as "fundamental" insofar as it seeks to protect the keeping and bearing of arms for private self-defense purposes. Nor can I find any justification for interpreting the Constitution as transferring ultimate regulatory authority over the private uses of firearms from democratically elected legislatures to courts or from the States to the Federal Government. I therefore conclude that the Fourteenth Amendment does not "incorporate" the Second Amend-ment's right "to keep and bear Arms." And I consequently dissent.

In my view, taking *Heller* as a given, the Fourteenth Amendment does not incorporate the Second Amendment right to keep and bear arms for purposes of private self-defense. Under this Court's precedents, to incor-porate the private self-defense right the majority must show that the right is, *e.g.,* "fundamental to the American scheme of justice." And this it fails to do.

The majority here, like that in *Heller,* relies almost exclusively upon history to make the necessary showing. But to do so for incorporation purposes is both wrong and dangerous. As Justice Stevens points out, our society has historically made mistakes—for example, when considering certain 18th- and 19th-century property rights to be fundamental. And in the incorporation context, as elsewhere, history often is unclear about the answers.

Accordingly, this Court, in considering an incorporation question, has never stated that the historical status of a right is the only relevant consideration. Rather, the Court has either explicitly or implicitly made clear in its opinions that the right in question has remained fundamental over time.

I thus think it proper, above all where history provides no clear answer, to look to other factors in considering whether a right is suffi-ciently "fundamental" to remove it from the political process in every State. I would include among those factors the nature of the right; any contemporary disagreement about whether the right is fundamental; the extent to which incorporation will further other, perhaps more basic, constitutional aims; and the extent to which incorporation will advance or hinder the Constitution's structural aims, including its division of powers among different governmental institutions (and the people as well). Is incorporation needed, for example, to further the Constitution's effort to ensure that the government treats each individual with equal respect? Will it help maintain the democratic form of government that the Constitution foresees? In a word, will incorporation prove consistent, or inconsistent, with the Constitution's efforts to create governmental institutions well suited to the carrying out of its constitutional promises?

Finally, I would take account of the Framers' basic reason for believing the Court ought to have the power of judicial review. Alexander Hamilton feared granting that power to Congress alone, for he feared that Congress, acting as judges, would not overturn as unconstitutional a popular statute that it had recently enacted, as legislators. That being so, it makes sense to ask whether that particular comparative judicial advantage is relevant to the case at hand.

How do these considerations apply here? For one thing, I would apply them only to the private self-defense right directly at issue. After all, the Amendment's militia-related purpose is primarily to protect *States* from *federal* regulation, not to protect individuals from militia-related regulation. Moreover, the Civil War Amendments, the electoral process, the courts, and numerous other institutions today help to safeguard the States and the people from any serious threat of federal tyranny. How are state militias additionally necessary? It is difficult to see how a right that, as the majority concedes, has "largely faded as a popular concern" could possibly be so fundamental that it would warrant incorporation through the Fourteenth Amendment. Hence, the incorporation of the Second Amendment cannot be based on the militia-related aspect of what *Heller* found to be more extensive Second Amendment rights.

For another thing, as *Heller* concedes, the private self-defense right that the Court would incorporate has nothing to do with "the *reason*" the Framers "codified" the right to keep and bear arms "in a written Constitution." *Heller* immediately adds that the self-defense right was nonetheless "the *central component* of the right." *Ibid.* In my view, this is the historical equivalent of a claim that water runs uphill. But, taking it as valid, the Framers' basic *reasons* for including language in the Constitution would nonetheless seem more pertinent (in deciding about the contemporary *importance* of a right) than the particular *scope* 17th- or 18th-century listeners would have then assigned to the words they used. And examination of the Framers' motivation tells us they did not think the private armed self-defense right was of paramount importance.

Further, there is no popular consensus that the private self-defense right described in *Heller* is fundamental. The plurality suggests that two *amici* briefs filed in the case show such a consensus, but, of course, numerous *amici* briefs have been filed opposing incorporation as well. Moreover, every State regulates firearms extensively, and public opinion is sharply divided on the appropriate level of regulation. Much of this disagreement rests upon empirical considerations. One side believes the right essential to protect the lives of those attacked in the home; the other side believes it essential to regulate the right in order to protect the lives of others attacked with guns. It seems unlikely that definitive evidence will develop one way or the other. And the appropriate level of firearm regulation has thus long been, and continues to be, a hotly contested matter of political debate. Finally, incorporation of the right *will* work a significant disruption in the constitutional allocation of decisionmaking authority, thereby interfering with the Constitution's ability to further its objectives.

In sum, the police power, the superiority of legislative decisionmaking, the need for local decisionmaking, the comparative desirability of democratic decisionmaking, the lack of a manageable judicial standard, and the life-threatening harm that may flow from striking down regulations all argue against incorporation. Where the incorporation of other rights has been at issue, *some* of these problems have arisen. But in this instance *all* these problems are present, *all* at the same time, and *all* are likely to be present in most, perhaps nearly all, of the cases in which the constitutionality of a gun regulation is at issue. At the same time, the important factors that favor incorporation in other instances— *e.g.,* the protection of broader constitutional objectives—are not present here. The upshot is that all factors militate against incorporation—with the possible exception of historical factors.

[T]he Framers did not write the Second Amendment in order to protect a private right of armed self-defense. There has been, and is, no consensus that the right is, or was, "fundamental." No broader constitutional interest or principle supports legal treatment of that right as fundamental. To the contrary, broader constitutional concerns of an institutional nature argue strongly against that treatment.

Moreover, nothing in 18th-, 19th-, 20th-, or 21st-century history shows a consensus that the right to private armed self-defense, as described in *Heller,* is "deeply rooted in this Nation's history or tradition" or is otherwise "fundamental." Indeed, incorporating the right recognized in *Heller* may change the law in many of the 50 States. Read in the majority's favor, the historical evidence is at most ambiguous. And, in the absence of any other support for its conclusion, ambiguous history cannot show that the Fourteenth Amendment incorporates a private right of self-defense against the States.

Chapter 8

Fundamental Rights Under Due Process and Equal Protection

L. Procedural Due Process

2. What Procedures Are Required? (casebook, p. 1197)

During October Term 2008, the Court decided two important cases concerning procedural due process. One, *Caperton v. Massey Coal Co.* involved whether due process is violated when a judge has received substantial contributions from a litigant. The other, *District Attorney's Office for the Third Judicial District v. Osborne*, involved whether due process required access to DNA testing for convicted criminal defendants. This case involved both procedural and substantive due process claims. Although the cases arise in very different contexts, they both concern what due process requires.

CAPERTON v. A.T. MASSEY COAL CO., INC.
129 S.Ct. 2252 (2009)

Justice KENNEDY delivered the opinion of the Court.

In this case the Supreme Court of Appeals of West Virginia reversed a trial court judgment, which had entered a jury verdict of $50 million. Five justices heard the case, and the vote to reverse was 3 to 2. The question presented is whether the Due Process Clause of the Fourteenth Amendment was violated when one of the justices in the majority denied a recusal motion. The basis for the motion was that the justice had received campaign contributions in an extraordinary amount from, and through the efforts of, the board chairman and principal officer of the corporation found liable for the damages.

Under our precedents there are objective standards that require recusal when "the probability of actual bias on the part of the judge or decision-maker is too high to be constitutionally tolerable." Applying those precedents, we find that, in all the circumstances of this case, due process requires recusal.

I

In August 2002 a West Virginia jury returned a verdict that found respondents A.T. Massey Coal Co. and its affiliates (hereinafter Massey) liable for fraudulent misrepresentation, concealment, and tortious interference with existing contractual relations. The jury awarded petitioners Hugh Caperton, Harman Development Corp., Harman Mining Corp., and Sovereign Coal Sales (hereinafter Caperton) the sum of $50 million in compensatory and punitive damages.

In June 2004 the state trial court denied Massey's post-trial motions challenging the verdict and the damages award, finding that Massey "intentionally acted in utter disregard of [Caperton's] rights and ultimately destroyed
[Caperton's] businesses because, after conducting cost-benefit analyses, [Massey] concluded it was in its financial interest to do so."

Don Blankenship is Massey's chairman, chief executive officer, and president. After the verdict but before the appeal, West Virginia held its 2004 judicial elections. Knowing the Supreme Court of Appeals of West Virginia would consider the appeal in the case, Blankenship decided to support an attorney who sought to replace Justice McGraw. Justice McGraw was a candidate for reelection to that court. The attorney who sought to replace him was Brent Benjamin.

In addition to contributing the $1,000 statutory maximum to Benjamin's campaign committee, Blankenship donated almost $2.5 million to "And For The Sake Of The Kids," a political organization formed under 26 U.S.C. § 527. The § 527 organization opposed McGraw and supported Benjamin. Blankenship's donations accounted for more than two-thirds of the total funds it raised. This was not all. Blankenship spent, in addition, just over $500,000 on independent expenditures—for direct mailings and letters soliciting donations as well as television and newspaper advertisements " 'to support . . . Brent Benjamin.' "

To provide some perspective, Blankenship's $3 million in contributions were more than the total amount spent by all other Benjamin supporters and three times the amount spent by Benjamin's own committee. Caperton contends that Blankenship spent $1 million more than the total amount spent by the campaign committees of both candidates combined.

Benjamin won. He received 382,036 votes (53.3%), and McGraw received 334,301 votes (46.7%).

In October 2005, before Massey filed its petition for appeal in West Virginia's highest court, Caperton moved to disqualify now-Justice Benjamin under the Due Process Clause and the West Virginia Code of Judicial Conduct, based on the conflict caused by Blankenship's campaign involvement. Justice Benjamin denied the motion in April 2006. He indicated that he "carefully considered the bases and accompanying exhibits proffered by the movants." But he found "no objective information . . . to show that this Justice has a bias for or against any litigant, that this Justice has prejudged the matters which comprise this litigation, or that this Justice will be anything but fair and impartial." In December 2006 Massey filed its petition for appeal to challenge the adverse jury verdict. The West Virginia Supreme Court of Appeals granted review.

In November 2007 that court reversed the $50 million verdict against Massey. The majority opinion, authored by then-Chief Justice Davis and joined by Justices Benjamin and Maynard, found that "Massey's conduct warranted the type of judgment rendered in this case." It reversed, nevertheless, based on two independent grounds—first, that a forum-selection clause contained in a contract to which Massey was not a party barred the suit in West Virginia, and, second, that res judicata barred the suit due to an out-of-state judgment to which Massey was not a party.

Caperton sought rehearing, and the parties moved for disqualification of three of the five justices who decided the appeal. Photos had surfaced of Justice Maynard vacationing with Blankenship in the French Riviera while the case was pending. Justice Maynard granted Caperton's recusal motion. On the other side Justice Starcher granted Massey's recusal motion, apparently based on his public criticism of Blankenship's role in the 2004 elections. In his recusal memorandum Justice Starcher urged Justice Benjamin to recuse himself as well. He noted that "Blankenship's bestowal of his personal wealth, political tactics, and 'friendship' have created a cancer in the affairs of this Court." Justice Benjamin declined Justice Starcher's suggestion and denied Caperton's recusal motion.

The court granted rehearing. Justice Benjamin, now in the capacity of acting chief justice, selected Judges Cookman and Fox to replace the recused justices. Caperton moved a third time for disqualification, arguing that Justice Benjamin had failed to apply the correct standard under West Virginia law—*i.e.,* whether "a reasonable and prudent person, knowing these objective facts, would harbor doubts about Justice Benjamin's ability to be fair and impartial." Caperton also included the results of a public opinion poll, which indicated that over 67% of West Virginians doubted Justice Benjamin would be fair and impartial. Justice Benjamin again refused to withdraw, noting that the "push poll" was "neither credible nor sufficiently reliable to serve as the basis for an elected judge's disqualification."

In April 2008 a divided court again reversed the jury verdict, and again it was a 3-to-2 decision. Justice Davis filed a modified version of her prior opinion, repeating the two earlier holdings. She was joined by Justice Benjamin and Judge Fox. Justice Albright, joined by Judge Cookman, dissented. The dissent also noted "genuine due process implications arising under federal law" with respect to Justice Benjamin's failure to recuse himself.

II

It is axiomatic that "[a] fair trial in a fair tribunal is a basic requirement of due process." As the Court has recognized, however, "most matters relating to judicial disqualification [do] not rise to a constitutional level." The early and leading case on the subject is *Tumey v. Ohio* (1927). There, the Court stated that "matters of kinship, personal bias, state policy, remoteness of interest, would seem generally to be matters merely of legislative discretion."

The *Tumey* Court concluded that the Due Process Clause incorporated the common-law rule that a judge must recuse himself when he has "a direct, personal, substantial, pecuniary interest" in a case. This rule reflects the maxim that "[n]o man is allowed to be a judge in his own cause; because his interest would certainly bias his judgment, and, not improbably, corrupt his integrity." The Federalist No. 10, p. 59 (J. Cooke ed.1961) (J. Madison). Under this rule, "disqualification for bias or prejudice was not permitted"; those matters were left to statutes and judicial codes. Personal bias or prejudice "alone would not be sufficient basis for imposing a constitutional requirement under the Due Process Clause."

As new problems have emerged that were not discussed at common law, however, the Court has identified additional instances which, as an objective matter, require recusal. These are circumstances "in which experience teaches that the probability of actual bias on the part of the judge or decisionmaker is too high to be constitutionally tolerable." To place the present case in proper context, two instances where the Court has required recusal merit further discussion.

The first involved the emergence of local tribunals where a judge had a financial interest in the outcome of a case, although the interest was less than what would have been considered personal or direct at common law. This was the problem addressed in *Tumey*. There, the mayor of a village had the authority to sit as a judge (with no jury) to try those accused of violating a state law prohibiting the possession of alcoholic beverages. Inherent in this structure were two potential conflicts. First, the mayor received a salary supplement for performing judicial duties, and the funds for that compensation derived from the fines assessed in a case. No fines were assessed upon acquittal. The mayor-judge thus received a salary supplement only if he convicted the defendant. Second, sums from the criminal fines were deposited to the village's general treasury fund for village improvements and repairs.

The Court held that the Due Process Clause required disqualification "both because of [the mayor-judge's] direct pecuniary interest in the outcome, and because of his official motive to convict and to graduate the fine to help the financial needs of the village." It so held despite observing that "[t]here are doubtless mayors who would not allow such a consideration as $12 costs in each case to affect their judgment in it." The Court articulated the controlling principle: "Every procedure which would offer a possible temptation to the average man as a judge to forget the burden of proof required to convict the defendant, or which might lead him not to hold the balance nice, clear and true between the State and the accused, denies the latter due process of law."

The Court was thus concerned with more than the traditional common-law prohibition on direct pecuniary interest. It was also concerned with a more general concept of interests that tempt adjudicators to disregard neutrality.

This concern with conflicts resulting from financial incentives was elaborated in *Ward v. Monroeville* (1972), which invalidated a conviction in another mayor's court. In *Monroeville,* unlike in *Tumey,* the mayor received no money; instead, the fines the mayor assessed went to the town's general fisc. The Court held that "[t]he fact that the mayor [in *Tumey*] shared directly in the fees and costs did not define the limits of the principle." The principle, instead, turned on the "possible temptation" the mayor might face; the mayor's "executive responsibilities for village finances may make him partisan to maintain the high level of contribution [to those finances] from the mayor's court."

The second instance requiring recusal that was not discussed at common law emerged in the criminal contempt context, where a judge had no pecuniary interest in the case but was challenged because of a conflict arising from his participation in an earlier proceeding. This Court characterized that first proceeding (perhaps pejoratively) as a " 'one-man grand jury.' "

In that first proceeding, and as provided by state law, a judge examined witnesses to determine whether criminal charges should be brought. The judge called the two petitioners before him. One petitioner answered questions, but the judge found him untruthful and charged him with perjury. The second declined to answer on the ground that he did not have counsel with him, as state law seemed to permit. The judge charged him with contempt. The judge proceeded to try and convict both petitioners.

This Court set aside the convictions on grounds that the judge had a conflict of interest at the trial stage because of his earlier participation followed by his decision to charge them. The Due Process Clause required disqualification. The Court recited the general rule that "no man can be a judge in his own case," adding that "no man is permitted to try cases where he has an interest in the outcome." It noted that the disqualifying criteria "cannot be defined with precision. Circumstances and relationships must be considered." These circumstances and the prior relationship required recusal: "Having been a part of [the one-man grand jury] process a judge cannot be, in the very nature of things, wholly disinterested in the conviction or acquittal of those accused." That is because "[a]s a practical matter it is difficult if not impossible for a judge to free himself from the influence of what took place in his 'grand-jury' secret session."

III

Based on the principles described in these cases we turn to the issue before us. This problem arises in the context of judicial elections, a framework not presented in the precedents we have reviewed and discussed.

Caperton contends that Blankenship's pivotal role in getting Justice Benjamin elected created a constitutionally intolerable probability of actual bias. Though not a bribe or criminal influence, Justice Benjamin would nevertheless feel a debt of gratitude to Blankenship for his extraordinary efforts to get him elected.

Justice Benjamin was careful to address the recusal motions and explain his reasons why, on his view of the controlling standard, disqualification was not in order. In four separate opinions issued during the course of the appeal, he explained why no actual bias had been established.

Following accepted principles of our legal tradition respecting the proper performance of judicial functions, judges often inquire into their subjective motives and purposes in the ordinary course of deciding a case. This does not mean the inquiry is a simple one. The difficulties of inquiring into actual bias, and the fact that the inquiry is often a private one, simply underscore the need for objective rules. Otherwise there may be no adequate protection against a judge who simply misreads or misapprehends the real motives at work in deciding the case. The judge's own inquiry into actual bias, then, is not one that the law can easily superintend or review, though actual bias, if disclosed, no doubt would be grounds for appropriate relief. In lieu of exclusive reliance on that personal inquiry, or on appellate review of the judge's determination respecting actual bias, the Due Process Clause has been implemented by objective standards that do not require proof of actual bias. In defining these standards the Court has asked whether, "under a realistic appraisal of psychological tendencies and human weakness," the interest "poses such a risk of actual bias or prejudgment that the practice must be forbidden if the guarantee of due process is to be adequately implemented."

We turn to the influence at issue in this case. Not every campaign contribution by a litigant or attorney creates a probability of bias that requires a judge's recusal, but this is an exceptional case. We conclude that there is a serious risk of actual bias—based on objective and reasonable perceptions—when a person with a personal stake in a particular case had a significant and disproportionate influence in placing the judge on the case by raising funds or directing the judge's election campaign when the case was pending or imminent. The inquiry centers on the contribution's relative size in comparison to the total amount of money contributed to the campaign, the total amount spent in the election, and the apparent effect such contribution had on the outcome of the election.

Applying this principle, we conclude that Blankenship's campaign efforts had a significant and disproportionate influence in placing Justice Benjamin on the case. Blankenship contributed some $3 million to unseat the incumbent and replace him with Benjamin. His contributions eclipsed the total amount spent by all other Benjamin supporters and exceeded by 300% the amount spent by Benjamin's campaign committee. Caperton claims Blankenship spent $1 million more than the total amount spent by the campaign committees of both candidates combined.

Massey responds that Blankenship's support, while significant, did not cause Benjamin's victory. In the end the people of West Virginia elected him, and they did so based on many reasons other than Blankenship's efforts. Massey points out that every major state newspaper, but one, endorsed Benjamin. It also contends that then-Justice McGraw cost himself the election by giving a speech during the campaign, a speech the opposition seized upon for its own advantage.

Whether Blankenship's campaign contributions were a necessary and sufficient cause of Benjamin's victory is not the proper inquiry. Much like determining whether a judge is actually biased, proving what ultimately drives the electorate to choose a particular candidate is a difficult endeavor, not likely to lend itself to a certain conclusion. This is particularly true where, as here, there is no procedure for judicial factfinding and the sole trier of fact is the one accused of bias. Due process requires an objective inquiry into whether the contributor's influence on the election under all the circumstances "would offer a possible temptation to the average . . . judge to . . . lead him not to hold the balance nice, clear and true." In an election decided by fewer than 50,000 votes (382,036 to 334,301), Blankenship's campaign contributions—in comparison to the total amount contributed to the campaign, as well as the total amount spent in the election—had a significant and disproportionate influence on the electoral outcome. And the risk that Blankenship's influence engendered actual bias is sufficiently substantial that it "must be forbidden if the guarantee of due process is to be adequately implemented."

The temporal relationship between the campaign contributions, the justice's election, and the pendency of the case is also critical. It was reasonably foreseeable, when the campaign contributions were made, that the pending case would be before the newly elected justice. The $50 million adverse jury verdict had been entered before the election, and the Supreme Court of Appeals was the next step once the state trial court dealt with post-trial motions. So it became at once apparent that, absent recusal, Justice Benjamin would review a judgment that cost his biggest donor's company $50 million. Although there is no allegation of a *quid pro quo* agreement, the fact remains that Blankenship's extraordinary contributions were made at a time when he had a vested stake in the outcome. Just as no man is allowed to be a judge in his own cause, similar fears of bias can arise when—without the consent of the other parties—a man chooses the judge in his own cause. And applying this principle to the judicial election process, there was here a serious, objective risk of actual bias that required Justice Benjamin's recusal.

Justice Benjamin did undertake an extensive search for actual bias. But, as we have indicated, that is just one step in the judicial process; objective standards may also require recusal whether or not actual bias exists or can be proved. Due process "may sometimes bar trial by judges who have no actual bias and who would do their very best to weigh the scales of justice equally between contending parties." The failure to consider objective standards requiring recusal is not consistent with the imperatives of due process. We find that Blankenship's significant and disproportionate influence—coupled with the temporal relationship between the election and the pending case "offer a possible temptation to the average . . . judge to . . . lead him not to hold the balance nice, clear and true." On these extreme facts the probability of actual bias rises to an unconstitutional level.

IV

Our decision today addresses an extraordinary situation where the Constitution requires recusal. Massey and its *amici* predict that various adverse consequences will follow from recognizing a constitutional violation here—ranging from a flood of recusal motions to unnecessary interference with judicial elections. We disagree. The facts now before us are extreme by any measure. The parties point to no other instance involving judicial campaign contributions that presents a potential for bias comparable to the circumstances in this case.

"The Due Process Clause demarks only the outer boundaries of judicial disqualifications. Congress and the states, of course, remain free to impose more rigorous standards for judicial disqualification than those we find mandated here today." Because the codes of judicial conduct provide more protection than due process requires, most disputes over disqualification will be resolved without resort to the Constitution. Application of the constitutional standard implicated in this case will thus be confined to rare instances.

Chief Justice ROBERTS, with whom Justice SCALIA, Justice THOMAS, and Justice ALITO join, dissenting.

I, of course, share the majority's sincere concerns about the need to maintain a fair, independent, and impartial judiciary—and one that appears to be such. But I fear that the Court's decision will undermine rather than promote these values.

Until today, we have recognized exactly two situations in which the Federal Due Process Clause requires disqualification of a judge: when the judge has a financial interest in the outcome of the case, and when the judge is trying a defendant for certain criminal contempts. Vaguer notions of bias or the appearance of bias were never a basis for disqualification, either at common law or under our constitutional precedents. Those issues were instead addressed by legislation or court rules.

Today, however, the Court enlists the Due Process Clause to overturn a judge's failure to recuse because of a "probability of bias." Unlike the established grounds for disqualification, a "probability of bias" cannot be defined in any limited way. The Court's new "rule" provides no guidance to judges and litigants about when recusal will be constitutionally required. This will inevitably lead to an increase in allegations that judges are biased, however groundless those charges may be. The end result will do far more to erode public confidence in judicial impartiality than an isolated failure to recuse in a particular case.

I

There is a "presumption of honesty and integrity in those serving as adjudicators." All judges take an oath to uphold the Constitution and apply the law impartially, and we trust that they will live up to this promise. Subject to the two well-established exceptions described above, questions of judicial recusal are regulated by "common law, statute, or the professional standards of the bench and bar."

In any given case, there are a number of factors that could give rise to a "probability" or "appearance" of bias: friendship with a party or lawyer, prior employment experience, membership in clubs or associations, prior speeches and writings, religious affiliation, and countless other considerations. We have never held that the Due Process Clause requires recusal for any of these reasons, even though they could be viewed as presenting a "probability of bias." Many state *statutes* require recusal based on a probability or appearance of bias, but "that alone would not be sufficient basis for imposing a *constitutional* requirement under the Due Process Clause." States are, of course, free to adopt broader recusal rules than the Constitution requires—and every State has—but these developments are not continuously incorporated into the Due Process Clause.

II

In departing from this clear line between when recusal is constitutionally required and when it is not, the majority repeatedly emphasizes the need for an "objective" standard. The majority's analysis is "objective" in that it does not inquire into Justice Benjamin's motives or decisionmaking process. But the standard the majority articulates—"probability of bias"—fails to provide clear, workable guidance for future cases. At the most basic level, it is unclear whether the new probability of bias standard is somehow limited to financial support in judicial elections, or applies to judicial recusal questions more generally.

But there are other fundamental questions as well. With little help from the majority, courts will now have to determine:

1. How much money is too much money? What level of contribution or expenditure gives rise to a "probability of bias"?
2. How do we determine whether a given expenditure is "disproportionate"? Disproportionate *to what*?
3. Are independent, non-coordinated expenditures treated the same as direct contributions to a candidate's campaign? What about contributions to independent outside groups supporting a candidate?
4. Does it matter whether the litigant has contributed to other candidates or made large expenditures in connection with other elections?
5. Does the amount at issue in the case matter? What if this case were an employment dispute with only $10,000 at stake? What if the plaintiffs only sought non-monetary relief such as an injunction or declaratory judgment?
6. Does the analysis change depending on whether the judge whose disqualification is sought sits on a trial court, appeals court, or state supreme court?
7. How long does the probability of bias last? Does the probability of bias diminish over time as the election recedes? Does it matter whether the judge plans to run for reelection?
8. What if the "disproportionately" large expenditure is made by an industry association, trade union, physicians' group, or the plaintiffs' bar? Must the judge recuse in all cases that affect the association's interests? Must the judge recuse in all cases in which a party or lawyer is a member of that group? Does it matter how much the litigant contributed to the association?
9. What if the case involves a social or ideological issue rather than a financial one? Must a judge recuse from cases involving, say, abortion rights if he has received "disproportionate" support from individuals who feel strongly about either side of that issue? If the supporter wants to help elect judges who are "tough on crime," must the judge recuse in all criminal cases?
10. What if the candidate draws "disproportionate" support from a particular racial, religious, ethnic, or other group, and the case involves an issue of particular importance to that group?
11. What if the supporter is not a party to the pending or imminent case, but his interests will be affected by the decision? Does the Court's analysis apply if the supporter "chooses the judge" not in *his* case, but in someone else's?

12. What if the case implicates a regulatory issue that is of great importance to the party making the expenditures, even though he has no direct financial interest in the outcome (*e.g.,* a facial challenge to an agency rulemaking or a suit seeking to limit an agency's jurisdiction)?

13. Must the judge's vote be outcome determinative in order for his non-recusal to constitute a due process violation?

14. Does the due process analysis consider the underlying merits of the suit? Does it matter whether the decision is clearly right (or wrong) as a matter of state law?

15. What if a lower court decision in favor of the supporter is affirmed on the merits on appeal, by a panel with no "debt of gratitude" to the supporter? Does that "moot" the due process claim?

16. What if the judge voted against the supporter in many other cases?

17. What if the judge disagrees with the supporter's message or tactics? What if the judge expressly *disclaims* the support of this person?

18. Should we assume that elected judges feel a "debt of hostility" towards major *opponents* of their candidacies? Must the judge recuse in cases involving individuals or groups who spent large amounts of money trying unsuccessfully to defeat him?

19. If there is independent review of a judge's recusal decision, *e.g.,* by a panel of other judges, does this completely foreclose a due process claim?

20. Does a debt of gratitude for endorsements by newspapers, interest groups, politicians, or celebrities also give rise to a constitutionally unacceptable probability of bias? How would we measure whether such support is disproportionate?

21. Does close personal friendship between a judge and a party or lawyer now give rise to a probability of bias?

22. Does it matter whether the campaign expenditures come from a party or the party's attorney? If from a lawyer, must the judge recuse in every case involving that attorney?

23. Does what is unconstitutional vary from State to State? What if particular States have a history of expensive judicial elections?

24. Under the majority's "objective" test, do we analyze the due process issue through the lens of a reasonable person, a reasonable lawyer, or a reasonable judge?

25. What role does causation play in this analysis? The Court sends conflicting signals on this point. The majority asserts that "[w]hether Blankenship's campaign contributions were a necessary and sufficient cause of Benjamin's victory is not the proper inquiry." But elsewhere in the opinion, the majority considers "the apparent effect such contribution had on the outcome of the election," and whether the litigant has been able to "choos[e] the judge in his own cause." If causation is a pertinent factor, how do we know whether the contribution or expenditure had any effect on the outcome of the election? What if the judge won in a landslide? What if the judge won primarily because of his opponent's missteps?

26. Is the due process analysis less probing for incumbent judges—who typically have a great advantage in elections—than for challengers?

27. How final must the pending case be with respect to the contributor's interest? What if, for example, the only issue on appeal is whether the court should certify a class of plaintiffs? Is recusal required just as if the issue in the pending case were ultimate liability?

28. Which cases are implicated by this doctrine? Must the case be pending at the time of the election? Reasonably likely to be brought? What about an important but unanticipated case filed shortly after the election?

29. When do we impute a probability of bias from one party to another? Does a contribution from a corporation get imputed to its executives, and vice-versa? Does a contribution or expenditure by one family member get imputed to other family members?

30. What if the election is nonpartisan? What if the election is just a yes-or-no vote about whether to retain an incumbent?

31. What type of support is disqualifying? What if the supporter's expenditures are used to fund voter registration or get-out-the-vote efforts rather than television advertisements?

32. Are contributions or expenditures in connection with a primary aggregated with those in the general election? What if the contributor supported a different candidate in the primary? Does that dilute the debt of gratitude?

33. What procedures must be followed to challenge a state judge's failure to recuse? May *Caperton* claims only be raised on direct review? Or may such claims also be brought in federal district court under 42 U.S.C. § 1983, which allows a person deprived of a federal right by a state official to sue for damages? If § 1983 claims are available, who are the proper defendants? The judge? The whole court? The clerk of court?

34. What about state-court cases that are already closed? Can the losing parties in those cases now seek collateral relief in federal district court under § 1983? What statutes of limitation should be applied to such suits?

35. What is the proper remedy? After a successful *Caperton* motion, must the parties start from scratch before the lower courts? Is any part of the lower court judgment retained?

36. Does a litigant waive his due process claim if he waits until after decision to raise it? Or would the claim only be ripe after decision, when the judge's actions or vote suggest a probability of bias?

37. Are the parties entitled to discovery with respect to the judge's recusal decision?

38. If a judge erroneously fails to recuse, do we apply harmless-error review?

39. Does the *judge* get to respond to the allegation that he is probably biased, or is his reputation solely in the hands of the parties to the case?

40. What if the parties settle a *Caperton* claim as part of a broader settlement of the case? Does that leave the judge with no way to salvage his reputation?

These are only a few uncertainties that quickly come to mind. Judges and litigants will surely encounter others when they are forced to, or wish to, apply the majority's decision in different circumstances. Today's opinion requires state and federal judges simultaneously to act as political scientists (why did candidate X win the election?), economists (was the financial support disproportionate?), and psychologists (is there likely to be a debt of gratitude?).

The Court's inability to formulate a "judicially discernible and manageable standard" strongly counsels against the recognition of a novel constitutional right.

III

To its credit, the Court seems to recognize that the inherently boundless nature of its new rule poses a problem. But the majority's only answer is that the present case is an "extreme" one, so there is no need to worry about other cases.

But this is just so much whistling past the graveyard. Claims that have little chance of success are nonetheless frequently filed. The success rate for certiorari petitions before this Court is approximately 1.1%, and yet the previous Term some 8,241 were filed. Every one of the "*Caperton* motions" or appeals or § 1983 actions will claim that the judge is biased, or probably biased, bringing the judge and the judicial system into disrepute. And all future litigants will assert that their case is *really* the most extreme thus far.

Extreme cases often test the bounds of established legal principles. There is a cost to yielding to the desire to correct the extreme case, rather than adhering to the legal principle. That cost has been demonstrated so often that it is captured in a legal aphorism: "Hard cases make bad law."

The déjà vu is enough to make one swoon. Today, the majority again departs from a clear, longstanding constitutional rule to accommodate an "extreme" case involving "grossly disproportionate" amounts of money. I believe we will come to regret this decision as well, when courts are forced to deal with a wide variety of *Caperton* motions, each claiming the title of "most extreme" or "most disproportionate."

B

And why is the Court so convinced that this is an extreme case? It is true that Don Blankenship spent a large amount of money in connection with this election. But this point cannot be emphasized strongly enough: Other than a $1,000 direct contribution from Blankenship, *Justice*

Benjamin and his campaign had no control over how this money was spent. Campaigns go to great lengths to develop precise messages and strategies. An insensitive or ham-handed ad campaign by an independent third party might distort the campaign's message or cause a backlash against the candidate, even though the candidate was not responsible for the ads.

Moreover, Blankenship's independent expenditures do not appear "grossly disproportionate" compared to other such expenditures in this very election. "And for the Sake of the Kids"—an independent group that received approximately two-thirds of its funding from Blankenship—spent $3,623,500 in connection with the election. But large independent expenditures were also made in support of Justice Benjamin's opponent. "Consumers for Justice"—an independent group that received large contributions from the plaintiffs' bar—spent approximately $2 million in this race. And Blankenship has made large expenditures in connection with several previous West Virginia elections, which undercuts any notion that his involvement in this election was "intended to influence the outcome" of particular pending litigation.

It is also far from clear that Blankenship's expenditures affected the outcome of this election. Justice Benjamin won by a comfortable 7-point margin (53.3% to 46.7%). Many observers believed that Justice Benjamin's opponent doomed his candidacy by giving a well-publicized speech that made several curious allegations; this speech was described in the local media as "deeply disturbing" and worse. Justice Benjamin's opponent also refused to give interviews or participate in debates. All but one of the major West Virginia newspapers endorsed Justice Benjamin. Justice Benjamin just might have won because the voters of West Virginia thought he would be a better judge than his opponent. Unlike the majority, I cannot say with any degree of certainty that Blankenship "cho[se] the judge in his own cause." I would give the voters of West Virginia more credit than that.

It is an old cliché, but sometimes the cure is worse than the disease. I am sure there are cases where a "probability of bias" should lead the prudent judge to step aside, but the judge fails to do so. Maybe this is one of them. But I believe that opening the door to recusal claims under the Due Process Clause, for an amorphous "probability of bias," will itself bring our judicial system into undeserved disrepute, and diminish the confidence of the American people in the fairness and integrity of their courts. I hope I am wrong. . . .

DISTRICT ATTORNEY'S OFFICE FOR THE
THIRD JUDICIAL DISTRICT v. OSBORNE
129 S.Ct. 2308 (2009)

Chief Justice ROBERTS delivered the opinion of the Court.

DNA testing has an unparalleled ability both to exonerate the wrongly convicted and to identify the guilty. It has the potential to significantly improve both the criminal justice system and police investigative practices. The Federal Government and the States have recognized this, and have developed special approaches to ensure that this evidentiary tool can be effectively incorporated into established criminal procedure—usually but not always through legislation.

Against this prompt and considered response, the respondent, William Osborne, proposes a different approach: the recognition of a freestanding and far-reaching constitutional right of access to this new type of evidence. This approach would take the development of rules and procedures in this area out of the hands of legislatures and state courts shaping policy in a focused manner and turn it over to federal courts applying the broad parameters of the Due Process Clause. There is no reason to constitutionalize the issue in this way. Because the decision below would do just that, we reverse.

I

This lawsuit arose out of a violent crime committed 16 years ago, which has resulted in a long string of litigation in the state and federal courts. On the evening of March 22, 1993, two men driving through Anchorage, Alaska, solicited sex from a female prostitute, K.G. She agreed to perform fellatio on both men for $100 and got in their car. The three spent some time looking for a place to stop and ended up in a deserted area near Earthquake Park. When K.G. demanded payment in advance, the two men pulled out a gun and forced her to perform fellatio on the driver while the passenger penetrated her vaginally, using a blue condom she had brought. The passenger then ordered K.G. out of the car and told her to lie face-down in the snow. Fearing for her life, she refused, and the two men choked her and beat her with the gun. When K.G. tried to flee, the passenger beat her with a wooden axe handle and shot her in the head while she lay on the ground. They kicked some snow on top of her and left her for dead.

K.G. did not die; the bullet had only grazed her head. Once the two men left, she found her way back to the road, and flagged down a passing car to take her home. Ultimately, she received medical care and spoke to the police. At the scene of the crime, the police recovered a spent shell casing, the axe handle, some of K.G.'s clothing stained with blood, and the blue condom.

Six days later, two military police officers at Fort Richardson pulled over Dexter Jackson for flashing his headlights at another vehicle. In his car they discovered a gun (which matched the shell casing), as well as several items K.G. had been carrying the night of the attack. The car also matched the description K.G. had given to the police. Jackson admitted that he had been the driver during the rape and assault, and told the police that William Osborne had been his passenger. Other evidence also implicated Osborne. K.G. picked out his photograph (with some uncertainty) and at trial she identified Osborne as her attacker. Other witnesses testified that shortly before the crime, Osborne had called Jackson from an arcade, and then driven off with him. An axe handle similar to the one at the scene of the crime was found in Osborne's room on the military base where he lived.

The State also performed DQ Alpha testing on sperm found in the blue condom. DQ Alpha testing is a relatively inexact form of DNA testing that can clear some wrongly accused individuals, but generally cannot narrow the perpetrator down to less than 5% of the population. The semen found on the condom had a genotype that matched a blood sample taken from Osborne, but not ones from Jackson, K. G., or a third suspect named James Hunter. Osborne is black, and approximately 16% of black individuals have such a genotype. App. 117-119. In other words, the testing ruled out Jackson and Hunter as possible sources of the semen, and also ruled out over 80% of other black individuals. The State also examined some pubic hairs found at the scene of the crime, which were not susceptible to DQ Alpha testing, but which state witnesses attested to be similar to Osborne's.

Osborne and Jackson were convicted by an Alaska jury of kidnapping, assault, and sexual assault. They were acquitted of an additional count of sexual assault and of attempted murder. Finding it "nearly miraculous" that K.G. had survived, the trial judge sentenced Osborne to 26 years in prison, with 5 suspended. His conviction and sentence were affirmed on appeal. Osborne then sought postconviction relief in Alaska state court. He claimed that he had asked his attorney, Sidney Billingslea, to seek more discriminating restriction-fragment-length-polymorphism (RFLP) DNA testing during trial, and argued that she was constitutionally ineffective for not doing so. In two decisions, the Alaska Court of Appeals concluded that Osborne had no right to the RFLP test. The court relied heavily on the fact that Osborne had confessed to some of his crimes in a 2004 application for parole—in which it is a crime to lie. In this statement, Osborne acknowledged forcing K.G. to have sex at gunpoint, as well as beating her and covering her with snow. He repeated this confession before the parole board.

II

Modern DNA testing can provide powerful new evidence unlike anything known before. Since its first use in criminal investigations in the mid-1980s, there have been several major advances in DNA technology, culminating in STR technology. It is now often possible to determine whether a biological tissue matches a suspect with near certainty. While of course many criminal trials proceed without any forensic and scientific testing at all, there is no technology comparable to DNA testing for matching tissues when such evidence is at issue. DNA testing has exonerated wrongly convicted people, and has confirmed the convictions of many others.

At the same time, DNA testing alone does not always resolve a case. Where there is enough other incriminating evidence and an explanation for the DNA result, science alone cannot prove a prisoner innocent. The availability of technologies not available at trial cannot mean that every criminal conviction, or even every criminal conviction involving biological evidence, is suddenly in doubt. The dilemma is how to harness DNA's power to prove innocence without unnecessarily overthrowing the established system of criminal justice.

That task belongs primarily to the legislature. "[T]he States are currently engaged in serious, thoughtful examinations," of how to ensure the fair and effective use of this testing within the existing criminal justice framework. Forty-six States have already enacted statutes dealing specifically with access to DNA evidence. The State of Alaska itself is considering joining them. The Federal Government has also passed the Innocence Protection Act of 2004, which allows federal prisoners to move for court-ordered DNA testing under certain specified conditions.

These laws recognize the value of DNA evidence but also the need for certain conditions on access to the State's evidence. A requirement of demonstrating materiality is common, but it is not the only one. The federal statute, for example, requires a sworn statement that the applicant is innocent. This requirement is replicated in several state statutes. States also impose a range of diligence requirements. Several require the requested testing to "have been technologically impossible at trial."

Others deny testing to those who declined testing at trial for tactical reasons.

Alaska is one of a handful of States yet to enact legislation specifically addressing the issue of evidence requested for DNA testing. But that does not mean that such evidence is unavailable for those seeking to prove their innocence. Instead, Alaska courts are addressing how to apply existing laws for discovery and postconviction relief to this novel technology. [T]he Alaska Court of Appeals has invoked a widely accepted three-part test to govern additional rights to DNA access under the State Constitution. Drawing on the experience with DNA evidence of State Supreme Courts around the country, the Court of Appeals explained that it was "reluctant to hold that Alaska law offers no remedy to defendants who could prove their factual innocence." It was "prepared to hold, however, that a defendant who seeks post-conviction DNA testing . . . must show (1) that the conviction rested primarily on eyewitness identification evidence, (2) that there was a demonstrable doubt concerning the defendant's identification as the perpetrator, and (3) that scientific testing would likely be conclusive on this issue." Thus, the Alaska courts have suggested that even those who do not get discovery under the State's criminal rules have available to them a safety valve under the State Constitution.

[III]

"No State shall . . . deprive any person of life, liberty, or property, without due process of law." This Clause imposes procedural limitations on a State's power to take away protected entitlements. Osborne argues that access to the State's evidence is a "process" needed to vindicate his right to prove himself innocent and get out of jail. Process is not an end in itself, so a necessary premise of this argument is that he has an entitlement (what our precedents call a "liberty interest") to prove his innocence even after a fair trial has proved otherwise. We must first examine this asserted liberty interest to determine what process (if any) is due.

In identifying his potential liberty interest, Osborne first attempts to rely on the Governor's constitutional authority to "grant pardons, commutations, and reprieves." That claim can be readily disposed of. We have held that noncapital defendants do not have a liberty interest in traditional state executive clemency, to which no particular claimant is *entitled* as a matter of state law. Osborne therefore cannot challenge the constitutionality of any procedures available to vindicate an interest in state clemency.

Osborne does, however, have a liberty interest in demonstrating his innocence with new evidence under state law. As explained, Alaska law provides that those who use "newly discovered evidence" to "establis[h] by clear and convincing evidence that [they are] innocent" may obtain "vacation of [their] conviction or sentence in the interest of justice." This "state-created right can, in some circumstances, beget yet other rights to procedures essential to the realization of the parent right."

A criminal defendant proved guilty after a fair trial does not have the same liberty interests as a free man. At trial, the defendant is presumed innocent and may demand that the government prove its case beyond reasonable doubt. But

"[o]nce a defendant has been afforded a fair trial and convicted of the offense for which he was charged, the presumption of innocence disappears." "Given a valid conviction, the criminal defendant has been constitutionally deprived of his liberty."

The State accordingly has more flexibility in deciding what procedures are needed in the context of postconviction relief. "[W]hen a State chooses to offer help to those seeking relief from convictions," due process does not "dictat[e] the exact form such assistance must assume." Osborne's right to due process is not parallel to a trial right, but rather must be analyzed in light of the fact that he has already been found guilty at a fair trial, and has only a limited interest in postconviction relief. *Brady* is the wrong framework.

Instead, the question is whether consideration of Osborne's claim within the framework of the State's procedures for postconviction relief "offends some principle of justice so rooted in the traditions and conscience of our people as to be ranked as fundamental," or "transgresses any recognized principle of fundamental fairness in operation."

We see nothing inadequate about the procedures Alaska has provided to vindicate its state right to postconviction relief in general, and nothing inadequate about how those procedures apply to those who seek access to DNA evidence. Alaska provides a substantive right to be released on a sufficiently compelling showing of new evidence that establishes innocence. It exempts such claims from otherwise applicable time limits. The State provides for discovery in postconviction proceedings, and has—through judicial decision—specified that this discovery procedure is available to those seeking access to DNA evidence. These procedures are not without limits. The evidence must indeed be newly available to qualify under Alaska's statute, must have been diligently pursued, and must also be sufficiently material. These procedures are similar to those provided for DNA evidence by federal law and the law of other States and they are not inconsistent with the "traditions and conscience of our people" or with "any recognized principle of fundamental fairness." And there is more. While the Alaska courts have not had occasion to conclusively decide the question, the Alaska Court of Appeals has suggested that the State Constitution provides an additional right of access to DNA. In expressing its "reluctan[ce] to hold that Alaska law offers no remedy" to those who belatedly seek DNA testing, and in invoking the three-part test used by other state courts, the court indicated that in an appropriate case the State Constitution may provide a failsafe even for those who cannot satisfy the statutory requirements under general post-conviction procedures.

The Court of Appeals below relied only on procedural due process, but Osborne seeks to defend the judgment on the basis of substantive due process as well. He asks that we recognize a freestanding right to DNA evidence untethered from the liberty interests he hopes to vindicate with it. We reject the invitation and conclude, in the circumstances of this case, that there is no such substantive due process right. "As a general matter, the Court has always been reluctant to expand the concept of substantive due process because guideposts for responsible decisionmaking in this unchartered area are scarce and open-ended." Osborne seeks access to state evidence so that he can apply new DNA-testing technology that might prove him innocent. There is no long history of such a right, and "[t]he mere novelty of such a claim is reason enough to doubt that 'substantive due process' sustains it."

And there are further reasons to doubt. The elected governments of the States are actively confronting the challenges DNA technology poses to our criminal justice systems and our traditional notions of finality, as well as the opportunities it affords. To suddenly constitutionalize this area would short-circuit what looks to be a prompt and considered legislative response. The first DNA testing statutes were passed in 1994 and 1997. In the past decade, 44 States and the Federal Government have followed suit, reflecting the increased availability of DNA testing. As noted, Alaska itself is considering such legislation. "By extending constitutional protection to an asserted right or liberty interest, we, to a great extent, place the matter outside the arena of public debate and legislative action. We must therefore exercise the utmost care whenever we are asked to break new ground in this field." "[J]udicial imposition of a categorical remedy . . . might pretermit other responsible solutions being considered in Congress and state legislatures." If we extended substantive due process to this area, we would cast these statutes into constitutional doubt and be forced to take over the issue of DNA access ourselves. We are reluctant to enlist the

Federal Judiciary in creating a new constitutional code of rules for handling DNA.

Establishing a freestanding right to access DNA evidence for testing would force us to act as policymakers, and our substantive-due-process rulemaking authority would not only have to cover the right of access but a myriad of other issues. We would soon have to decide if there is a constitutional obligation to preserve forensic evidence that might later be tested. If so, for how long? Would it be different for different types of evidence? Would the State also have some obligation to gather such evidence in the first place? How much, and when? No doubt there would be a miscellany of other minor directives.

DNA evidence will undoubtedly lead to changes in the criminal justice system. It has done so already. The question is whether further change will primarily be made by legislative revision and judicial interpretation of the existing system, or whether the Federal Judiciary must leap ahead—revising (or even discarding) the system by creating a new constitutional right and taking over responsibility for refining it.

Federal courts should not presume that state criminal procedures will be inadequate to deal with technological change. The criminal justice system has historically accommodated new types of evidence, and is a time-tested means of carrying out society's interest in convicting the guilty while respecting individual rights. That system, like any human endeavor, cannot be perfect. DNA evidence shows that it has not been. But there is no basis for Osborne's approach of assuming that because DNA has shown that these procedures are not flawless, DNA evidence must be treated as categorically outside the process, rather than within it.

Justice STEVENS, with whom Justice GINSBURG and Justice BREYER join, and with whom Justice SOUTER joins as to Part I, dissenting.

The State of Alaska possesses physical evidence that, if tested, will conclusively establish whether respondent William Osborne committed rape and attempted murder. If he did, justice has been served by his conviction and sentence. If not, Osborne has needlessly spent decades behind bars while the true culprit has not been brought to justice. The DNA test Osborne seeks is a simple one, its cost modest, and its results uniquely precise. Yet for reasons the State has been unable or unwilling to articulate, it refuses to allow Osborne to test the evidence at his own expense and to thereby ascertain the truth once and for all.

Because I am convinced that Osborne has a constitutional right of access to the evidence he wishes to test and that, on the facts of this case, he has made a sufficient showing of entitlement to that evidence, I would affirm the decision of the Court of Appeals.

Osborne asserts a right to access the State's evidence that derives from the Due Process Clause itself. Whether framed as a "substantive liberty interest ... protected through a procedural due process right" to have evidence made available for testing, or as a substantive due process right to be free of arbitrary government action, the result is the same: On the record now before us, Osborne has established his entitlement to test the State's evidence.

The liberty protected by the Due Process Clause is not a creation of the Bill of Rights. Indeed, our Nation has long recognized that the liberty safeguarded by the Constitution has far deeper roots.

Although a valid criminal conviction justifies punitive detention, it does not entirely eliminate the liberty interests of convicted persons. For while a prisoner's "rights may be diminished by the needs and exigencies of the institutional environment[,] ... [t]here is no iron curtain drawn between the Constitution and the prisons of this country." It is therefore far too late in the day to question the basic proposition that convicted persons such as Osborne retain a constitutionally protected measure of interest in liberty, including the fundamental liberty of freedom from physical restraint.

Recognition of this right draws strength from the fact that 46 States and the Federal Government have passed statutes providing access to evidence for DNA testing, and 3 additional states (including Alaska) provide similar access through court-made rules alone.These legislative developments are consistent with recent trends in legal ethics recognizing that prosecutors are obliged to disclose all forms of exculpatory evidence that come into their possession following conviction. The fact that nearly all the States have now recognized some postconviction right to DNA evidence makes it more, not less, appropriate to recognize a limited federal right to such evidence in cases where litigants are unfairly barred from obtaining relief in state court.

Recent scientific advances in DNA analysis have made "it literally possible to confirm guilt or innocence beyond any question whatsoever, at least in some categories of cases." As the Court recognizes today, the powerful new evidence that modern DNA testing can provide is "unlike anything known before."

If the right Osborne seeks to vindicate is framed as purely substantive, the proper result is no less clear. "The touchstone of due process is protection of the individual against arbitrary action of government." When government action is so lacking in justification that it "can properly be characterized as arbitrary, or conscience shocking, in a constitutional sense," it violates the Due Process Clause. In my view, the State's refusal to provide Osborne with access to evidence for DNA testing qualifies as arbitrary.

Throughout the course of state and federal litigation, the State has failed to provide any concrete reason for denying Osborne the DNA testing he seeks, and none is apparent. Because Osborne has offered to pay for the tests, cost is not a factor. And as the State now concedes, there is no reason to doubt that such testing would provide conclusive confirmation of Osborne's guilt or revelation of his innocence. In the courts below, the State refused to provide an explanation for its refusal to permit testing of the evidence, and in this Court, its explanation has been, at best, unclear. Insofar as the State has articulated any reason at all, it appears to be a generalized interest in protecting the finality of the judgment of conviction from any possible future attacks.

While we have long recognized that States have an interest in securing the finality of their judgments, finality is not a stand-alone value that trumps a State's overriding interest in ensuring that justice is done in its courts and secured to its citizens. Indeed, when absolute proof of innocence is readily at hand, a State should not shrink from the possibility that error may have occurred. Rather, our system of justice is strengthened by "recogniz[ing] the need for, and imperative of, a safety valve in those rare instances where objective proof that the convicted actually did not commit the offense later becomes available through the progress of science."

This conclusion draws strength from the powerful state interests that offset the State's purported interest in finality *per se*. When a person is convicted for a crime he did not commit, the true culprit escapes punishment. DNA testing may lead to his identification. Crime victims, the law enforcement profession, and society at large share a strong interest in identifying and apprehending the actual perpetrators of vicious crimes, such as the rape and attempted murder that gave rise to this case.

The arbitrariness of the State's conduct is highlighted by comparison to the private interests it denies. It seems to me obvious that if a wrongly convicted person were to produce proof of his actual innocence, no state interest would be sufficient to justify his continued punitive detention. If such proof can be readily obtained without imposing a significant burden on the State, a refusal to provide access to such evidence is wholly unjustified.

In sum, an individual's interest in his physical liberty is one of constitutional significance. That interest would be vindicated by providing postconviction access to DNA evidence, as would the State's interest in ensuring that it punishes the true perpetrator of a crime. In this case, the State has suggested no countervailing interest that justifies its refusal to allow Osborne to test the evidence in its possession and has not provided any other nonarbitrary explanation for its conduct. Consequently, I am left to conclude that the State's failure to provide Osborne access to the evidence constitutes arbitrary action that offends basic principles of due process.

Chapter 9

First Amendment: Freedom of Expression

B. Free Speech Methodology

1. The Distinction Between Content-Based and Content-Neutral Laws

c. Problems in Applying the Distinction Between Content-Based and Content-Neutral Laws (casebook, p. 1232)

In *Pleasant Grove City, Utah v. Summum,* the Supreme Court held that the government may engage in content-based discrimination when the government is the speaker. The Court held this in the context of the government adopting a privately donated monument as its own speech. The question will be whether this will open the door to the government engaging in content-based discrimination by adopting other private speech as government expression.

PLEASANT GROVE CITY, UTAH v. SUMMUM
129 S.Ct. 1125 (2009)

Justice ALITO delivered the opinion of the Court.

This case presents the question whether the Free Speech Clause of the First Amendment entitles a private group to insist that a municipality permit it to place a permanent monument in a city park in which other donated monuments were previously erected. The Court of Appeals held that the municipality was required to accept the monument because a public park is a traditional public forum. We conclude, however, that although a park is a traditional public forum for speeches and other transitory expressive acts, the display of a permanent monument in a public park is not a form of expression to which forum analysis applies.

Instead, the placement of a permanent monument in a public park is best viewed as a form of government speech and is therefore not subject to scrutiny under the Free Speech Clause.

I

Pioneer Park (or Park) is a 2.5 acre public park located in the Historic District of Pleasant Grove City (or City) in Utah. The Park currently contains 15 permanent displays, at least 11 of which were donated by private groups or individuals. These include an historic granary, a wishing well, the City's first fire station, a September 11 monument, and a Ten Commandments monument donated by the Fraternal Order of Eagles in 1971.

Respondent Summum is a religious organization founded in 1975 and headquartered in Salt Lake City, Utah. On two separate occasions in 2003, Summum's president wrote a letter to the City's mayor requesting permission to erect a "stone monument," which would contain "the Seven Aphorisms of SUMMUM" and be similar in size and nature to the Ten Commandments monument. The City denied the requests.

In May 2005, respondent's president again wrote to the mayor asking to erect a monument, but the letter did not describe the monument, its historical significance, or Summum's connection to the community. The city council rejected this request.

In 2005, respondent filed this action against the City and various local officials (petitioners), asserting, among other claims, that petitioners had violated the Free Speech Clause of the First Amendment by accepting the Ten Commandments monument but rejecting the proposed Seven Aphorisms monument.

II

No prior decision of this Court has addressed the application of the Free Speech Clause to a government entity's acceptance of privately donated, permanent monuments for installation in a public park, and the parties disagree sharply about the line of precedents that governs this situation. The parties' fundamental disagreement thus centers on the nature of petitioners' conduct when they permitted privately donated monuments to be erected in Pioneer Park. Were petitioners engaging in their own expressive conduct? Or were they providing a forum for private speech?

If petitioners were engaging in their own expressive conduct, then the Free Speech Clause has no application. The Free Speech Clause restricts government regulation of private speech; it does not regulate government speech. Indeed, it is not easy to imagine how government could function if it lacked this freedom. "If every citizen were to have a right to insist that no one paid by public funds express a view with which he disagreed, debate over issues of great concern to the public would be limited to those in the private sector, and the process of government as we know it radically transformed."

A government entity may exercise this same freedom to express its views when it receives assistance from private sources for the purpose of delivering a government-controlled message.

This does not mean that there are no restraints on government speech. For example, government speech must comport with the Establishment Clause. The involvement of public officials in advocacy may be limited by law, regulation, or practice. And of course, a government entity is ultimately "accountable to the electorate and the political process for its advocacy."

While government speech is not restricted by the Free Speech Clause, the government does not have a free hand to regulate private speech on government property. This Court long ago recognized that members of the public retain strong free speech rights when they venture into public streets and parks, "which 'have immemorially been held in trust for the use of the public and, time out of mind, have been used for purposes of assembly, communicating thoughts between citizens, and discussing public questions.'" In order to preserve this freedom, government entities are strictly limited in their ability to regulate private speech in such "traditional public fora." Reasonable time, place, and manner restrictions are allowed, but any restriction based on the content of the speech must satisfy strict scrutiny, that is, the restriction must be narrowly tailored to serve a compelling government interest, and restrictions based on viewpoint are prohibited.

III

There may be situations in which it is difficult to tell whether a government entity is speaking on its own behalf or is providing a forum for private speech, but this case does not present such a situation. Permanent monuments displayed on public property typically represent government speech.

Governments have long used monuments to speak to the public. Since ancient times, kings, emperors, and other rulers have erected statues of themselves to remind their subjects of their authority and power. Triumphal arches, columns, and other monuments have been built to

commemorate military victories and sacrifices and other events of civic
importance. A monument, by definition, is a structure that is designed as
a means of expression. When a government entity arranges for the
construction of a monument, it does so because it wishes to convey
some thought or instill some feeling in those who see the structure.
Neither the Court of Appeals nor respondent disputes the obvious proposition that a monument that is commissioned and financed by a
government body for placement on public land constitutes government
speech.

Just as government-commissioned and government-financed monuments speak for the government, so do privately financed and donated
monuments that the government accepts and displays to the public on
government land. It certainly is not common for property owners to open
up their property for the installation of permanent monuments that
convey a message with which they do not wish to be associated. And
because property owners typically do not permit the construction of such
monuments on their land, persons who observe donated monuments
routinely—and reasonably—interpret them as conveying some message
on the property owner's behalf. In this context, there is little chance that
observers will fail to appreciate the identity of the speaker. This is true
whether the monument is located on private property or on public
property, such as national, state, or city park land.

Public parks are often closely identified in the public mind with the
government unit that owns the land. City parks ranging from those in
small towns, like Pioneer Park in Pleasant Grove City, to those in major
metropolises, like Central Park in New York City—commonly play an
important role in defining the identity that a city projects to its own
residents and to the outside world. Accordingly, cities and other jurisdictions take some care in accepting donated monuments. Government
decisionmakers select the monuments that portray what they view as
appropriate for the place in question, taking into account such content-
based factors as esthetics, history, and local culture. The monuments that
are accepted, therefore, are meant to convey and have the effect of
conveying a government message, and they thus constitute government
speech.

IV

In this case, it is clear that the monuments in Pleasant Grove's Pioneer
Park represent government speech. Although many of the monuments
were not designed or built by the City and were donated in completed

form by private entities, the City decided to accept those donations and to display them in the Park. Respondent does not claim that the City ever opened up the Park for the placement of whatever permanent monuments might be offered by private donors. Rather, the City has "effectively controlled" the messages sent by the monuments in the Park by exercising "final approval authority" over their selection. The City has selected those monuments that it wants to display for the purpose of presenting the image of the City that it wishes to project to all who frequent the Park; it has taken ownership of most of the monuments in the Park, including the Ten Commandments monument that is the focus of respondent's concern; and the City has now expressly set forth the criteria it will use in making future selections.

Respondent voices the legitimate concern that the government speech doctrine not be used as a subterfuge for favoring certain private speakers over others based on viewpoint. Respondent's suggested solution is to require a government entity accepting a privately donated monument to go through a formal process of adopting a resolution publicly embracing "the message" that the monument conveys.

We see no reason for imposing a requirement of this sort. The parks of this country contain thousands of donated monuments that government entities have used for their own expressive purposes, usually without producing the sort of formal documentation that respondent now says is required to escape Free Speech Clause restrictions. Requiring all of these jurisdictions to go back and proclaim formally that they adopt all of these monuments as their own expressive vehicles would be a pointless exercise that the Constitution does not mandate.

Contrary to respondent's apparent belief, it frequently is not possible to identify a single "message" that is conveyed by an object or structure, and consequently, the thoughts or sentiments expressed by a government entity that accepts and displays such an object may be quite different from those of either its creator or its donor. By accepting a privately donated monument and placing it on city property, a city engages in expressive conduct, but the intended and perceived significance of that conduct may not coincide with the thinking of the monument's donor or creator. Indeed, when a privately donated memorial is funded by many small donations, the donors themselves may differ in their interpretation of the monument's significance. By accepting such a monument, a government entity does not necessarily endorse the specific meaning that any particular donor sees in the monument.

Respondent and the Court of Appeals analogize the installation of permanent monuments in a public park to the delivery of speeches and the holding of marches and demonstrations, and they thus invoke the rule that a public park is a traditional public forum for these activities. But "public forum principles . . . are out of place in the context of this case." The forum doctrine has been applied in situations in which government-owned property or a government program was capable of accommodating a large number of public speakers without defeating the essential function of the land or the program. For example, a park can accommodate many speakers and, over time, many parades and demonstrations.

By contrast, public parks can accommodate only a limited number of permanent monuments. Public parks have been used, "'time out of mind, . . . for purposes of assembly, communicating thoughts between citizens, and discussing public questions,'" but "one would be hard pressed to find a 'long tradition' of allowing people to permanently occupy public space with any manner of monuments."

Speakers, no matter how long-winded, eventually come to the end of their remarks; persons distributing leaflets and carrying signs at some point tire and go home; monuments, however, endure. They monopolize the use of the land on which they stand and interfere permanently with other uses of public space. A public park, over the years, can provide a soapbox for a very large number of orators—often, for all who want to speak—but it is hard to imagine how a public park could be opened up for the installation of permanent monuments by every person or group wishing to engage in that form of expression.

If government entities must maintain viewpoint neutrality in their selection of donated monuments, they must either "brace themselves for an influx of clutter" or face the pressure to remove longstanding and cherished monuments. Every jurisdiction that has accepted a donated war memorial may be asked to provide equal treatment for a donated monument questioning the cause for which the veterans fought. New York City, having accepted a donated statue of one heroic dog (Balto, the sled dog who brought medicine to Nome, Alaska, during a diphtheria epidemic) may be pressed to accept monuments for other dogs who are claimed to be equally worthy of commemoration. The obvious truth of the matter is that if public parks were considered to be traditional public forums for the purpose of erecting privately donated monuments, most parks would have little choice but to refuse all such donations. And where the application of forum analysis would lead almost inexorably to closing of the forum, it is obvious that forum analysis is out of place.

To be sure, there are limited circumstances in which the forum doctrine might properly be applied to a permanent monument—for example, if a town created a monument on which all of its residents (or all those meeting some other criterion) could place the name of a person to be honored or some other private message. But as a general matter, forum analysis simply does not apply to the installation of permanent monuments on public property.

V

In sum, we hold that the City's decision to accept certain privately donated monuments while rejecting respondent's is best viewed as a form of government speech. As a result, the City's decision is not subject to the Free Speech Clause, and the Court of Appeals erred in holding otherwise. We therefore reverse.

Justice STEVENS, with whom Justice GINSBURG joins, concurring.

This case involves a property owner's rejection of an offer to place a permanent display on its land. While I join the Court's persuasive opinion, I think the reasons justifying the city's refusal would have been equally valid if its acceptance of the monument, instead of being characterized as "government speech," had merely been deemed an implicit endorsement of the donor's message. To date, our decisions relying on the recently minted government speech doctrine to uphold government action have been few and, in my view, of doubtful merit. The Court's opinion in this case signals no expansion of that doctrine. And by joining the Court's opinion, I do not mean to indicate agreement with our earlier decisions. Nor is it likely, given the near certainty that observers will associate permanent displays with the governmental property owner, that the government will be able to avoid political accountability for the views that it endorses or expresses through this means. Finally, recognizing permanent displays on public property as government speech will not give the government free license to communicate offensive or partisan messages. For even if the Free Speech Clause neither restricts nor protects government speech, government speakers are bound by the Constitution's other proscriptions, including those supplied by the Establishment and Equal Protection Clauses. Together with the checks imposed by our democratic processes, these constitutional safeguards ensure that the effect of today's decision will be limited.

Justice SCALIA, with whom Justice THOMAS joins, concurring.

As framed and argued by the parties, this case presents a question under the Free Speech Clause of the First Amendment. I agree with the

Court's analysis of that question and join its opinion in full. But it is also obvious that from the start, the case has been litigated in the shadow of the First Amendment's *Establishment* Clause: the city wary of associating itself too closely with the Ten Commandments monument displayed in the park, lest that be deemed a breach in the so-called "wall of separation between church and State."

The city ought not fear that today's victory has propelled it from the Free Speech Clause frying pan into the Establishment Clause fire. Contrary to respondent's intimations, there are very good reasons to be confident that the park displays do not violate *any* part of the First Amendment.

In *Van Orden v. Perry* (2005), this Court upheld against Establishment Clause challenge a virtually identical Ten Commandments monument, donated by the very same organization (the Fraternal Order of Eagles), which was displayed on the grounds surrounding the Texas State Capitol. Nothing in that decision suggested that the outcome turned on a finding that the monument was only "private" speech.

The city can safely exhale. Its residents and visitors can now return to enjoying Pioneer Park's wishing well, its historic granary—and, yes, even its Ten Commandments monument—without fear that they are complicit in an establishment of religion.

Justice BREYER, concurring.

I agree with the Court and join its opinion. I do so, however, on the understanding that the "government speech" doctrine is a rule of thumb, not a rigid category. Were the City to discriminate in the selection of permanent monuments on grounds unrelated to the display's theme, say solely on political grounds, its action might well violate the First Amendment.

In my view, courts must apply categories such as "government speech," "public forums," "limited public forums," and "nonpublic forums" with an eye towards their purposes—lest we turn "free speech" doctrine into a jurisprudence of labels. Consequently, we must sometimes look beyond an initial categorization. And, in doing so, it helps to ask whether a government action burdens speech disproportionately in light of the action's tendency to further a legitimate government objective.

Were we to do so here, we would find—for reasons that the Court sets forth—that the City's action, while preventing Summum from erecting its monument, does not disproportionately restrict Summum's freedom of expression. The City has not closed off its parks to speech; no one claims that the City prevents Summum's members from engaging in speech in a form more transient than a permanent monument. Rather, the City has simply reserved some space in the park for projects designed to further other than free-speech goals. And that is perfectly proper. After all, parks do not serve speech-related interests alone. To the contrary, cities use park space to further a variety of recreational, historical, educational, aesthetic, and other civic interests. To reserve to the City the power to pick and choose among proposed monuments according to criteria reasonably related to one or more of these legitimate ends restricts Summum's expression, but, given the impracticality of alternatives and viewed in light of the City's legitimate needs, the restriction is not disproportionate. Analyzed either way, as "government speech" or as a proportionate restriction on Summum's expression, the City's action here is lawful.

Justice SOUTER, concurring in the judgment.

I agree with the Court that the Ten Commandments monument is government speech, that is, an expression of a government's position on the moral and religious issues raised by the subject of the monument. And although the government should lose when the character of the speech is at issue and its governmental nature has not been made clear, I also agree with the Court that the city need not satisfy the particular formality urged by Summum as a condition of recognizing that the expression here falls within the public category. I have qualms, however, about accepting the position that public monuments are government speech categorically.

Because the government speech doctrine is "recently minted," it would do well for us to go slow in setting its bounds, which will affect existing doctrine in ways not yet explored.

The case shows that it may not be easy to work out. After today's decision, whenever a government maintains a monument it will presumably be understood to be engaging in government speech. If the monument has some religious character, the specter of violating the Establishment Clause will behoove it to take care to avoid the appearance of a flat-out establishment of religion, in the sense of the government's adoption of the tenets expressed or symbolized. In such an instance, there will be safety in numbers, and it will be in the interest of a careful government to accept other monuments to stand nearby, to dilute the appearance of adopting whatever particular religious position the single example alone might stand for. As mementoes and testimonials pile up, however, the chatter may well make it less intuitively obvious that the government is speaking in its own right simply by maintaining the monuments.

To avoid relying on a *per se* rule to say when speech is governmental, the best approach that occurs to me is to ask whether a reasonable and fully informed observer would understand the expression to be government speech, as distinct from private speech the government chooses to oblige by allowing the monument to be placed on public land. This reasonable observer test for governmental character is of a piece with the one for spotting forbidden governmental endorsement of religion in the Establishment Clause cases. The adoption of it would thus serve coherence within Establishment Clause law, and it would make sense of our common understanding that some monuments on public land display religious symbolism that clearly does not express a government's chosen views.

Application of this observer test provides the reason I find the monument here to be government expression.

2.   Vagueness and overbreadth

b.   *Overbreadth (casebook, p. 249)*

In *United States v. Stevens* (2010), the Court declared unconstitutional federal law that made it a crime to sell, distribute, or possess depictions of animal cruelty. The decision was based, in part, on a reluctance to create new categorical exceptions to the First Amendment, and, in part, on overbreadth grounds.

U.S. v. STEVENS
130 S.Ct. 1577 (2010)

Chief Justice ROBERTS delivered the opinion of the Court.

Congress enacted 18 U.S.C. § 48 to criminalize the commercial creation, sale, or possession of certain depictions of animal cruelty. The statute does not address underlying acts harmful to animals, but only portrayals of such conduct. The question presented is whether the prohibition in the statute is consistent with the freedom of speech guaranteed by the First Amendment.

I

Section 48 establishes a criminal penalty of up to five years in prison for anyone who knowingly "creates, sells, or possesses a depiction of animal cruelty," if done "for commercial gain" in interstate or foreign commerce. A depiction of "animal cruelty" is defined as one "in which a living animal is intentionally maimed, mutilated, tortured, wounded, or killed," if that conduct violates federal or state law where "the creation, sale, or possession takes place." In what is referred to as the "exceptions clause," the law exempts from prohibition any depiction "that has serious religious, political, scientific, educational, journalistic, historical, or artistic value."

The legislative background of § 48 focused primarily on the interstate market for "crush videos." According to the House Committee Report on the bill, such videos feature the intentional torture and killing of helpless animals, including cats, dogs, monkeys, mice, and hamsters. Crush videos often depict women slowly crushing animals to death "with their bare feet or while wearing high heeled shoes," sometimes while "talking to the animals in a kind of dominatrix patter" over "[t]he cries and squeals of the animals, obviously in great pain." Apparently these depictions "appeal to persons with a very specific sexual fetish who find them sexually arousing or otherwise exciting." The acts depicted in crush videos are typically prohibited by the animal cruelty laws enacted by all 50 States and the District of Columbia. But crush videos rarely disclose the participants' identities, inhibiting prosecution of the underlying conduct.

This case, however, involves an application of § 48 to depictions of animal fighting. Dogfighting, for example, is unlawful in all 50 States and the District of Columbia, and has been restricted by federal law since 1976. Respondent Robert J. Stevens ran a business, "Dogs of Velvet and Steel," and an associated Web site, through which he sold videos of pit bulls engaging in dogfights and attacking other animals.

Stevens moved to dismiss the indictment, arguing that § 48 is facially invalid under the First Amendment. The District Court denied the motion. It held that the depictions subject to § 48, like obscenity or child pornography, are categorically unprotected by the First Amendment. The jury convicted Stevens on all counts, and the District Court sentenced him to three concurrent sentences of 37 months' imprisonment, followed by three years of supervised release. The en banc Third Circuit, over a three-judge dissent, declared § 48 facially unconstitutional and vacated Stevens's conviction.

II

The Government's primary submission is that § 48 necessarily complies with the Constitution because the banned depictions of animal cruelty, as a class, are categorically unprotected by the First Amendment. We disagree.

"[A]s a general matter, the First Amendment means that government has no power to restrict expression because of its message, its ideas, its subject matter, or its content." Section 48 explicitly regulates expression based on content: The statute restricts "visual [and] auditory depiction[s]," such as photographs, videos, or sound recordings, depending on whether they depict conduct in which a living animal is intentionally harmed. As such, § 48 is "'presumptively invalid,' and the Government bears the burden to rebut that presumption."

"From 1791 to the present," however, the First Amendment has "permitted restrictions upon the content of speech in a few limited areas," and has never "include[d] a freedom to disregard these tradition-al limitations." These "historic and traditional categories long familiar to the bar," including obscenity, defamation, fraud, incitement, and speech integral to criminal conduct, are "well-defined and narrowly limited classes of speech, the prevention and punishment of which have never been thought to raise any Constitutional problem."

The Government argues that "depictions of animal cruelty" should be added to the list. It contends that depictions of "illegal acts of animal cruelty" that are "made, sold, or possessed for commercial gain" nec-essarily "lack expressive value," and may accordingly "be regulated as *unprotected* speech." The claim is not just that Congress may regulate depictions of animal cruelty subject to the First Amendment, but that these depictions are outside the reach of that Amendment altogether-that they fall into a "'First Amendment Free Zone.'"

As the Government notes, the prohibition of animal cruelty itself has a long history in American law, starting with the early settlement of the Colonies. But we are unaware of any similar tradition excluding *depic-tions* of animal cruelty from "the freedom of speech" codified in the First Amendment, and the Government points us to none.

The Government contends that "historical evidence" about the reach of the First Amendment is not "a necessary prerequisite for regulation today," and that categories of speech may be exempted from the First Amendment's protection without any long-settled tradition of subjecting that speech to regulation. Instead, the Government points to Congress's "'legislative judgment that . . . depictions of animals being intentionally tortured and killed [are] of such minimal redeeming value as to render [them] unworthy of First Amendment protection,'" and asks the Court to uphold the ban on the same basis. The Government thus proposes that a claim of categorical exclusion should be considered under a simple balancing test: "Whether a given category of speech enjoys First Amendment protection depends upon a categorical balancing of the value of the speech against its societal costs."

As a free-floating test for First Amendment coverage, that sentence is startling and dangerous. The First Amendment's guarantee of free speech does not extend only to categories of speech that survive an ad hoc balancing of relative social costs and benefits. The First Amendment itself reflects a judgment by the American people that the benefits of its restrictions on the Government outweigh the costs. Our Constitution forecloses any attempt to revise that judgment simply on the basis that some speech is not worth it.

When we have identified categories of speech as fully outside the protection of the First Amendment, it has not been on the basis of a simple cost-benefit analysis. In [*New York v.*] *Ferber,* for example, we classified child pornography as such a category. We noted that the State of New York had a compelling interest in protecting children from abuse, and that the value of using children in these works (as opposed to simulated conduct or adult actors) was *de minimis.* But our decision did not rest on this "balance of competing interests" alone. We made clear that *Ferber* presented a special case: The market for child pornography was "intrinsically related" to the underlying abuse, and was therefore "an integral part of the production of such materials, an activity illegal throughout the Nation." *Ferber* thus grounded its analysis in a previously recognized, long-established category of unprotected speech, and our subsequent decisions have shared this understanding.

Our decisions in *Ferber* and other cases cannot be taken as establishing a freewheeling authority to declare new categories of speech outside the scope of the First Amendment. Maybe there are some categories of speech that have been historically unprotected, but have not yet been specifically identified or discussed as such in our case law. But if so, there is no evidence that "depictions of animal cruelty" is among them. We need not foreclose the future recognition of such additional categories to reject the Government's highly manipulable balancing test as a means of identifying them.

III

Because we decline to carve out from the First Amendment any novel exception for § 48, we review Stevens's First Amendment challenge under our existing doctrine.

Stevens challenged § 48 on its face, arguing that any conviction secured under the statute would be unconstitutional. The court below decided the case on that basis.

To succeed in a typical facial attack, Stevens would have to establish "that no set of circumstances exists under which [§ 48] would be valid," or that the statute lacks any "plainly legitimate sweep." In the First Amendment context, however, this Court recognizes "a second type of facial challenge," whereby a law may be invalidated as overbroad if "a substantial number of its applications are unconstitutional, judged in relation to the statute's plainly legitimate sweep." Stevens argues that § 48 applies to common depictions of ordinary and lawful activities, and that these depictions constitute the vast majority of materials subject to the statute. The Government makes no effort to defend such a broad ban as constitutional. Instead, the Government's entire defense of § 48 rests on interpreting the statute as narrowly limited to specific types of "extreme" material. As the parties have presented the issue, therefore, the constitutionality of § 48 hinges on how broadly it is construed. It is to that question that we now turn.

As we explained two Terms ago, "[t]he first step in overbreadth analysis is to construe the challenged statute; it is impossible to determine whether a statute reaches too far without first knowing what the statute covers." We read § 48 to create a criminal prohibition of alarming breadth. To begin with, the text of the statute's ban on a "depiction of animal cruelty" nowhere requires that the depicted conduct be cruel. That text applies to "any . . . depiction" in which "a living animal is intentionally maimed, mutilated, tortured, wounded, or killed." "[M]aimed, mutilated, [and] tortured" convey cruelty, but "wounded" or "killed" do not suggest any such limitation.

The Government contends that the terms in the definition should be read to require the additional element of "accompanying acts of cruelty." But the phrase "wounded . . . or killed" at issue here contains little ambiguity. We agree that "wounded" and "killed" should be read according to their ordinary meaning. Nothing about that meaning requires cruelty.

While not requiring cruelty, § 48 does require that the depicted conduct be "illegal." But this requirement does not limit § 48 along the lines the Government suggests. There are myriad federal and state laws concerning the proper treatment of animals, but many of them are not designed to guard against animal cruelty. Protections of endangered species, for example, restrict even the humane "wound[ing] or kill[ing]" of "living animal[s]." Livestock regulations are often designed to protect the health of human beings, and hunting and fishing rules (seasons, licensure, bag limits, weight requirements) can be designed to raise revenue, preserve animal populations, or prevent accidents. The text of § 48(c) draws no distinction based on the reason the intentional killing of an animal is made illegal, and includes, for example, the humane slaughter of a stolen cow.

What is more, the application of § 48 to depictions of illegal conduct extends to conduct that is illegal in only a single jurisdiction. Under subsection (c)(1), the depicted conduct need only be illegal in "the State in which the creation, sale, or possession takes place, regardless of whether the . . . wounding . . . or killing took place in [that] State." A depiction of entirely lawful conduct runs afoul of the ban if that depiction later finds its way into another State where the same conduct is unlawful. This provision greatly expands the scope of § 48, because although there may be "a broad societal consensus" against cruelty to animals, there is substantial disagreement on what types of conduct are properly regarded as cruel. Both views about cruelty to animals and regulations having no connection to cruelty vary widely from place to place.

In the District of Columbia, for example, all hunting is unlawful. Other jurisdictions permit or encourage hunting, and there is an enormous national market for hunting-related depictions in which a living animal is intentionally killed. Hunting periodicals have circulations in the hundreds of thousands or millions, and hunting television programs, videos, and Web sites are equally popular. The demand for hunting depictions exceeds the estimated demand for crush videos or animal fighting depictions by several orders of magnitude.

Those seeking to comply with the law thus face a bewildering maze of regulations from at least 56 separate jurisdictions. Some States permit hunting with crossbows, while others forbid it, or restrict it only to the disabled. Missouri allows the "canned" hunting of ungulates held in captivity, but Montana restricts such hunting to certain bird species. The sharp-tailed grouse may be hunted in Idaho, but not in Washington. The disagreements among the States—and the "commonwealth[s], territor[ies], or possession[s] of the United States,"—extend well beyond hunting. State agricultural regulations permit different methods of livestock slaughter in different places or as applied to different animals.

The only thing standing between defendants who sell such depictions and five years in federal prison-other than the mercy of a prosecutor-is the statute's exceptions clause. Subsection (b) exempts from prohibition "any depiction that has serious religious, political, scientific, educational, journalistic, historical, or artistic value."

The Government's attempt to narrow the statutory ban, however, requires an unrealistically broad reading of the exceptions clause. But the text says "serious" value, and "serious" should be taken seriously. We decline the Government's invitation—advanced for the first time in this Court—to regard as "serious" anything that is not "scant."

Quite apart from the requirement of "serious" value in § 48(b), the excepted speech must also fall within one of the enumerated categories. Much speech does not. Most hunting videos, for example, are not obviously instructional in nature, except in the sense that all life is a lesson.

The Government explains that the language of § 48(b) was largely drawn from our opinion in *Miller v. California* (1973), which excepted from its definition of obscenity any material with "serious literary, artistic, political, or scientific value." According to the Government, this incorporation of the *Miller* standard into § 48 is therefore surely enough to answer any First Amendment objection.

We did not, however, determine that serious value could be used as a general precondition to protecting *other* types of speech in the first place. *Most* of what we say to one another lacks "religious, political, scientific, educational, journalistic, historical, or artistic value" (let alone serious value), but it is still sheltered from government regulation. Even "'[w]holly neutral futilities . . . come under the protection of free speech as fully as do Keats' poems or Donne's sermons.'" Thus, the protection of the First Amendment presumptively extends to many forms of speech that do not qualify for the serious-value exception of § 48(b), but nonetheless fall within the broad reach of § 48(c).

Not to worry, the Government says: The Executive Branch construes § 48 to reach only "extreme" cruelty, and it "neither has brought nor will bring a prosecution for anything less." The Government hits this theme hard, invoking its prosecutorial discretion several times. But the First Amendment protects against the Government; it does not leave us at the mercy of *noblesse oblige*. We would not uphold an unconstitutional statute merely because the Government promised to use it responsibly.

* * *

Nor does the Government seriously contest that the presumptively impermissible applications of § 48 (properly construed) far outnumber any permissible ones. However "growing" and "lucrative" the markets for crush videos and dogfighting depictions might be, they are dwarfed by the market for other depictions, such as hunting magazines and videos, that we have determined to be within the scope of § 48. We therefore need not and do not decide whether a statute limited to crush videos or other depictions of extreme animal cruelty would be constitutional. We hold only that § 48 is not so limited but is instead substantially overbroad, and therefore invalid under the First Amendment.

Justice ALITO, dissenting.

The Court strikes down in its entirety a valuable statute, 18 U.S.C. § 48, that was enacted not to suppress speech, but to prevent horrific acts of animal cruelty—in particular, the creation and commercial exploitation of "crush videos," a form of depraved entertainment that has no social value. The Court's approach, which has the practical effect of legalizing the sale of such videos and is thus likely to spur a resumption of their production, is unwarranted. Respondent was convicted under § 48 for selling videos depicting dogfights. On appeal, he argued, among other things, that § 48 is unconstitutional as applied to the facts of this case, and he highlighted features of those videos that might distinguish them from other dogfight videos brought to our attention.

Instead of applying the doctrine of overbreadth, I would vacate the decision below and instruct the Court of Appeals on remand to decide whether the videos that respondent sold are constitutionally protected. If the question of overbreadth is to be decided, however, I do not think the present record supports the Court's conclusion that § 48 bans a substantial quantity of protected speech.

In determining whether a statute's overbreadth is substantial, we consider a statute's application to real-world conduct, not fanciful hypotheticals. Accordingly, we have repeatedly emphasized that an overbreadth claimant bears the burden of demonstrating, "from the text of [the law] *and from actual fact,*" that substantial overbreadth exists. Similarly, "there must be a *realistic danger* that the statute itself will significantly compromise recognized First Amendment protections of parties not before the Court for it to be facially challenged on overbreadth grounds."

In holding that § 48 violates the overbreadth rule, the Court declines to decide whether, as the Government maintains, § 48 is constitutional as applied to two broad categories of depictions that exist in the real world: crush videos and depictions of deadly animal fights. Instead, the Court tacitly assumes for the sake of argument that § 48 is valid as applied to these depictions, but the Court concludes that § 48 reaches too much protected speech to survive. The Court relies primarily on depictions of hunters killing or wounding game and depictions of animals being slaughtered for food.

I turn first to depictions of hunting. As the Court notes, photographs and videos of hunters shooting game are common. But hunting is legal in all 50 States, and § 48 applies only to a depiction of conduct that is illegal in the jurisdiction in which the depiction is created, sold, or possessed. Therefore, in all 50 States, the creation, sale, or possession for sale of the vast majority of hunting depictions indisputably falls outside § 48's reach.

The Court's interpretation is seriously flawed. "When a federal court is dealing with a federal statute challenged as overbroad, it should, of course, construe the statute to avoid constitutional problems, if the statute is subject to such a limiting construction." Applying this canon, I would hold that § 48 does not apply to depictions of hunting. First, because § 48 targets depictions of "animal cruelty," I would interpret that term to apply only to depictions involving acts of animal cruelty as defined by applicable state or federal law, not to depictions of acts that happen to be illegal for reasons having nothing to do with the prevention of animal cruelty.

Second, even if the hunting of wild animals were otherwise covered by § 48(a), I would hold that hunting depictions fall within the exception in § 48(b) for depictions that have "serious" (*i.e.,* not "trifling") "scientific," "educational," or "historical" value. While there are certainly those who find hunting objectionable, the predominant view in this country has long been that hunting serves many important values, and it is clear that Congress shares that view. I do not have the slightest doubt that Congress, in enacting § 48, had no intention of restricting the creation, sale, or possession of depictions of hunting. Proponents of the law made this point clearly.

In sum, we have a duty to interpret § 48 so as to avoid serious constitutional concerns, and § 48 may reasonably be construed not to reach almost all, if not all, of the depictions that the Court finds constitutionally protected. Thus, § 48 does not appear to have a large number of unconstitutional applications. Invalidation for overbreadth is appropriate only if the challenged statute suffers from *substantial* overbreadth-judged not just in absolute terms, but in relation to the statute's "plainly legitimate sweep."

IV

It is undisputed that the *conduct* depicted in crush videos may constitutionally be prohibited. All 50 States and the District of Columbia have enacted statutes prohibiting animal cruelty. But before the enactment of

§ 48, the underlying conduct depicted in crush videos was nearly impossible to prosecute. These videos, which "often appeal to persons with a very specific sexual fetish," were made in secret, generally without a live audience, and "the faces of the women inflicting the torture in the material often were not shown, nor could the location of the place where the cruelty was being inflicted or the date of the activity be ascertained from the depiction." Thus, law enforcement authorities often were not able to identify the parties responsible for the torture.

In light of the practical problems thwarting the prosecution of the creators of crush videos under state animal cruelty laws, Congress concluded that the only effective way of stopping the underlying criminal conduct was to prohibit the commercial exploitation of the videos of that conduct. And Congress' strategy appears to have been vindicated. We are told that "[b]y 2007, sponsors of § 48 declared the crush video industry dead. Even overseas Websites shut down in the wake of § 48. Now, after the Third Circuit's decision [facially invalidating the statute], crush videos are already back online."

The First Amendment protects freedom of speech, but it most certainly does not protect violent criminal conduct, even if engaged in for expressive purposes. Crush videos present a highly unusual free speech issue because they are so closely linked with violent criminal conduct. The videos record the commission of violent criminal acts, and it appears that these crimes are committed for the sole purpose of creating the videos. In addition, as noted above, Congress was presented with compelling evidence that the only way of preventing these crimes was to target the sale of the videos. Under these circumstances, I cannot believe that the First Amendment commands Congress to step aside and allow the underlying crimes to continue.

The most relevant of our prior decisions is *Ferber v. New York* (1982), which concerned child pornography. The Court there held that child pornography is not protected speech, and I believe that *Ferber*'s reasoning dictates a similar conclusion here.

It must be acknowledged that § 48 differs from a child pornography law in an important respect: preventing the abuse of children is certainly much more important than preventing the torture of the animals used in crush videos. But while protecting children is unquestionably *more* important than protecting animals, the Government also has a compelling interest in preventing the torture depicted in crush videos.

The animals used in crush videos are living creatures that experience excruciating pain. Our society has long banned such cruelty, which is illegal throughout the country. In *Ferber,* the Court noted that "virtually all of the States and the United States have passed legislation proscribing the production of or otherwise combating 'child pornography,'" and the Court declined to "second-guess [that] legislative judgment."

In sum, § 48 may validly be applied to at least two broad real-world categories of expression covered by the statute: crush videos and dogfighting videos. Thus, the statute has a substantial core of constitutionally permissible applications. Moreover, for the reasons set forth above, the record does not show that § 48, properly interpreted, bans a substantial amount of protected speech in absolute terms. A *fortiori*, respondent has not met his burden of demonstrating that any impermissible applications of the statute are "substantial" in relation to its "plainly legitimate sweep." Accordingly, I would reject respondent's claim that § 48 is facially unconstitutional under the overbreadth doctrine.

4.   What is an infringement of freedom of speech?

Compelled speech (casebook, p. 1294)

In *McIntyre v. Ohio Election Commission* (casebook, p. 1303), the Court held that there is a First Amendment right to speak anonymously. In *Doe v. Reed* (2010), the Court considered whether it violates the First Amendment for a state to disclose the identity of those who sign a petition for a ballot referendum.

JOHN DOE NO. 1 v. REED
130 S.Ct. _____ (2010)

Chief Justice ROBERTS delivered the opinion of the Court.

The State of Washington allows its citizens to challenge state laws by referendum. Roughly four percent of Washington voters must sign a petition to place such a referendum on the ballot. That petition, which by law must include the names and addresses of the signers, is then submitted to the government for verification and canvassing, to ensure that only lawful signatures are counted. The Washington Public Records Act (PRA) authorizes private parties to obtain copies of government documents, and the State construes the PRA to cover submitted referendum petitions.

This case arises out of a state law extending certain benefits to same-sex couples, and a corresponding referendum petition to put that law to a popular vote. Respondent intervenors invoked the PRA to obtain copies of the petition, with the names and addresses of the signers. Certain petition signers and the petition sponsor objected, arguing that such public disclosure would violate their rights under the First Amendment.

The course of this litigation, however, has framed the legal question before us more broadly. The issue at this stage of the case is not whether disclosure of this particular petition would violate the First Amendment, but whether disclosure of referendum petitions in general would do so. We conclude that such disclosure does not as a general matter violate the First Amendment, and we therefore affirm the judgment of the Court of Appeals. We leave it to the lower courts to consider in the first instance the signers' more focused claim concerning disclosure of the information on this particular petition, which is pending before the District Court.

I

The Washington Constitution reserves to the people the power to reject any bill, with a few limited exceptions not relevant here, through the referendum process. To initiate a referendum, proponents must file a petition with the secretary of state that contains valid signatures of registered Washington voters equal to or exceeding four percent of the votes cast for the office of Governor at the last gubernatorial election. A valid submission requires not only a signature, but also the signer's address and the county in which he is registered to vote.

In May 2009, Washington Governor Christine Gregoire signed into law Senate Bill 5688, which "expand[ed] the rights and responsibilities" of state-registered domestic partners, including same-sex domestic partners. That same month, Protect Marriage Washington, one of the petitioners here, was organized as a "State Political Committee" for the purpose of collecting the petition signatures necessary to place a referendum on the ballot, which would give the voters themselves an opportunity to vote on SB 5688. If the referendum made it onto the ballot, Protect Marriage Washington planned to encourage voters to reject SB 5688.

On July 25, 2009, Protect Marriage Washington submitted to the secretary of state a petition containing over 137,000 signatures. The secretary of state then began the verification and canvassing process, as required by Washington law, to ensure that only legal signatures were counted. Some 120,000 valid signatures were required to place the referendum on the ballot. The secretary of state determined that the petition contained a sufficient number of valid signatures, and the referendum (R-71) appeared on the November 2009 ballot. The voters approved SB 5688 by a margin of 53% to 47%.

The [Public Records Act] makes all "public records" available for public inspection and copying. Washington takes the position that referendum petitions are "public records."

By August 20, 2009, the secretary had received requests for copies of the R-71 petition from an individual and four entities. The referendum petition sponsor and certain signers filed a complaint and a motion for a preliminary injunction in the United States District Court for the Western District of Washington, seeking to enjoin the secretary of state from publicly releasing any documents that would reveal the names and contact information of the R-71 petition signers. Count I of the complaint alleges that "[t]he Public Records Act is unconstitutional as applied to referendum petitions." Count II of the complaint alleges that "[t]he Public Records Act is unconstitutional as applied to the Referendum 71 petition because there is a reasonable probability that the signatories of the Referendum 71 petition will be subjected to threats, harassment, and reprisals." Determining that the PRA burdened core political speech, the District Court held that plaintiffs were likely to succeed on the merits of Count I and granted them a preliminary injunction on that count, enjoining release of the information on the petition.

The United States Court of Appeals for the Ninth Circuit reversed. Reviewing only Count I of the complaint, the Court of Appeals held that plaintiffs were unlikely to succeed on their claim that the PRA is unconstitutional as applied to referendum petitions generally. It therefore reversed the District Court's grant of the preliminary injunction.

[II]

The compelled disclosure of signatory information on referendum petitions is subject to review under the First Amendment. An individual expresses a view on a political matter when he signs a petition under Washington's referendum procedure. In most cases, the individual's signature will express the view that the law subject to the petition should be overturned. Even if the signer is agnostic as to the merits of the underlying law, his signature still expresses the political view that the question should be considered "by the whole electorate." In either case, the expression of a political view implicates a First Amendment right. The State, having "cho[sen] to tap the energy and the legitimizing power of the democratic process, . . . must accord the participants in that process the First Amendment rights that attach to their roles."

Petition signing remains expressive even when it has legal effect in the electoral process. But that is not to say that the electoral context is irrelevant to the nature of our First Amendment review. We allow States significant flexibility in implementing their own voting systems. To the extent a regulation concerns the legal effect of a particular activity in that process, the government will be afforded substantial latitude to enforce that regulation. Also pertinent to our analysis is the fact that the PRA is not a prohibition on speech, but instead a *disclosure* requirement. "[D]isclosure requirements may burden the ability to speak, but they . . . do not prevent anyone from speaking."

We have a series of precedents considering First Amendment challenges to disclosure requirements in the electoral context. These precedents have reviewed such challenges under what has been termed "exacting scrutiny." That standard "requires a 'substantial relation' between the disclosure requirement and a 'sufficiently important' governmental interest." To withstand this scrutiny, "the strength of the governmental interest must reflect the seriousness of the actual burden on First Amendment rights."

Respondents assert two interests to justify the burdens of compelled disclosure under the PRA on First Amendment rights: (1) preserving the integrity of the electoral process by combating fraud, detecting invalid signatures, and fostering government transparency and accountability; and (2) providing information to the electorate about who supports the petition. Because we determine that the State's interest in preserving the integrity of the electoral process suffices to defeat the argument that the PRA is unconstitutional with respect to referendum petitions in general, we need not, and do not, address the State's "informational" interest.

The State's interest in preserving the integrity of the electoral process is undoubtedly important. "States allowing ballot initiatives have considerable leeway to protect the integrity and reliability of the initiative process, as they have with respect to election processes generally." The State's interest is particularly strong with respect to efforts to root out fraud, which not only may produce fraudulent outcomes, but has a systemic effect as well: It "drives honest citizens out of the democratic process and breeds distrust of our government." The threat of fraud in this context is not merely hypothetical; respondents and their *amici* cite a number of cases of petition-related fraud across the country to support the point.

But the State's interest in preserving electoral integrity is not limited to combating fraud. That interest extends to efforts to ferret out invalid signatures caused not by fraud but by simple mistake, such as duplicate signatures or signatures of individuals who are not registered to vote in the State. That interest also extends more generally to promoting transparency and accountability in the electoral process, which the State argues is "essential to the proper functioning of a democracy."

Disclosure also helps prevent certain types of petition fraud otherwise difficult to detect, such as outright forgery and "bait and switch" fraud, in which an individual signs the petition based on a misrepresentation of the underlying issue. The signer is in the best position to detect these types of fraud, and public disclosure can bring the issue to the signer's attention.

Public disclosure thus helps ensure that the only signatures counted are those that should be, and that the only referenda placed on the ballot are those that garner enough valid signatures. Public disclosure also promotes transparency and accountability in the electoral process to an extent other measures cannot. In light of the foregoing, we reject plaintiffs' argument and conclude that public disclosure of referendum petitions in general is substantially related to the important interest of preserving the integrity of the electoral process.

Plaintiffs' more significant objection is that "the strength of the governmental interest" does not "reflect the seriousness of the actual burden on First Amendment rights." According to plaintiffs, the objective of those seeking disclosure of the R-71 petition is not to prevent fraud, but to publicly identify those who had validly signed and to broadcast the signers' political views on the subject of the petition. Plaintiffs allege, for example, that several groups plan to post the petitions in searchable form on the Internet, and then encourage other citizens to seek out the R-71 signers.

Plaintiffs explain that once on the Internet, the petition signers' names and addresses "can be combined with publicly available phone numbers and maps," in what will effectively become a blueprint for harassment and intimidation. To support their claim that they will be subject to reprisals, plaintiffs cite examples from the history of a similar proposition in California, and from the experience of one of the petition sponsors in this case.

In related contexts, we have explained that those resisting disclosure can prevail under the First Amendment if they can show "a reasonable probability that the compelled disclosure [of personal information] will subject them to threats, harassment, or reprisals from either Government officials or private parties." The question before us, however, is not whether PRA disclosure violates the First Amendment with respect to those who signed the R-71 petition, or other particularly controversial petitions. The question instead is whether such disclosure in general violates the First Amendment rights of those who sign referendum petitions.

The problem for plaintiffs is that their argument rests almost entirely on the specific harm they say would attend disclosure of the information on the R-71 petition, or on similarly controversial ones. But typical referendum petitions "concern tax policy, revenue, budget, or other state law issues." Voters care about such issues, some quite deeply—but there is no reason to assume that any burdens imposed by disclosure of typical referendum petitions would be remotely like the burdens plaintiffs fear in this case.

Plaintiffs have offered little in response. They have provided us scant evidence or argument beyond the burdens they assert disclosure would impose on R-71 petition signers or the signers of other similarly controversial petitions. Indeed, what little plaintiffs do offer with respect to typical petitions in Washington hurts, not helps: Several other petitions in the State "have been subject to release in recent years," plaintiffs tell us, but apparently that release has come without incident.

Faced with the State's unrebutted arguments that only modest burdens attend the disclosure of a typical petition, we must reject plaintiffs' broad challenge to the PRA. In doing so, we note—as we have in other election law disclosure cases—that upholding the law against a broad-based challenge does not foreclose a litigant's success in a narrower one. The secretary of state acknowledges that plaintiffs may press the narrower challenge in Count II of their complaint in proceedings pending before the District Court.

* * *

We conclude that disclosure under the PRA would not violate the First Amendment with respect to referendum petitions in general and therefore affirm the judgment of the Court of Appeals.

Justice ALITO, concurring.

The Court holds that the disclosure under the Washington Public Records Act (PRA), of the names and addresses of persons who sign referendum petitions does not as a general matter violate the First Amendment, and I agree with that conclusion. Nonetheless, facially valid disclosure requirements can impose heavy burdens on First Amendment rights in individual cases. Acknowledging that reality, we have long held that speakers can obtain as-applied exemptions from disclosure requirements if they can show "a reasonable probability that the compelled disclosure of [personal information] will subject them to threats, harassment, or reprisals from either Government officials or private parties." Because compelled disclosure can "burden the ability to speak," and "seriously infringe on privacy of association and belief guaranteed by the First Amendment," the as-applied exemption plays a critical role in safeguarding First Amendment rights.

The possibility of prevailing in an as-applied challenge provides adequate protection for First Amendment rights only if (1) speakers can obtain the exemption sufficiently far in advance to avoid chilling protected speech and (2) the showing necessary to obtain the exemption is not overly burdensome.

In light of those principles, the plaintiffs in this case have a strong argument that the PRA violates the First Amendment as applied to the Referendum 71 petition. Consider first the burdens on plaintiffs' First Amendment rights. The widespread harassment and intimidation suffered by supporters of California's Proposition 8 provides strong support for an as-applied exemption in the present case. Proposition 8 amended the California Constitution to provide that "[o]nly marriage between a man and a woman is valid or recognized in California," and plaintiffs submitted to the District Court substantial evidence of the harassment suffered by Proposition 8 supporters. Indeed, if the evidence relating to Proposition 8 is not sufficient to obtain an as-applied exemption in this case, one may wonder whether that vehicle provides any meaningful protection for the First Amendment rights of persons who circulate and sign referendum and initiative petitions.

As-applied challenges to disclosure requirements play a critical role in protecting First Amendment freedoms. To give speech the breathing room it needs to flourish, prompt judicial remedies must be available well before the relevant speech occurs and the burden of proof must be low. In this case-both through analogy and through their own experiences-plaintiffs have a strong case that they are entitled to as-applied relief, and they will be able to pursue such relief before the District Court.

Justice SOTOMAYOR with whom Justice STEVENS and Justice GINSBURG join, concurring.

In assessing the countervailing interests at stake in this case, we must be mindful of the character of initiatives and referenda. These mechanisms of direct democracy are not compelled by the Federal Constitution. It is instead up to the people of each State, acting in their sovereign capacity, to decide whether and how to permit legislation by popular action. States enjoy "considerable leeway" to choose the subjects that are eligible for placement on the ballot and to specify the requirements for obtaining ballot access (*e.g.,* the number of signatures required, the time for submission, and the method of verification). As the Court properly recognizes, each of these structural decisions "inevitably affects-at least to some degree-the individual's right" to speak about political issues and "to associate with others for political ends." For instance, requiring petition signers to be registered voters or to use their real names no doubt limits the ability or willingness of some individuals to undertake the expressive act of signing a petition. Regulations of this nature, however, stand "a step removed from the communicative aspect of petitioning," and the ability of States to impose them can scarcely be doubted.

The Court today confirms that the State of Washington's decision to make referendum petition signatures available for public inspection falls squarely within the realm of permissible election-related regulations. Public disclosure of the identity of petition signers, which is the rule in the overwhelming majority of States that use initiatives and referenda, advances States' vital interests in "[p]reserving the integrity of the electoral process, preventing corruption, and sustaining the active, alert responsibility of the individual citizen in a democracy for the wise conduct of government."

On the other side of the ledger, I view the burden of public disclosure on speech and associational rights as minimal in this context. As this Court has observed with respect to campaign-finance regulations, "disclosure requirements . . . 'do not prevent anyone from speaking.'" When it comes to initiatives and referenda, the impact of public disclosure on expressive interests is even more attenuated. While campaign-finance disclosure injects the government into what would otherwise have been private political activity, the process of legislating by referendum is inherently public. To qualify a referendum for the ballot, citizens are required to sign a petition and supply identifying information to the State. The act of signing typically occurs in public, and the circulators who collect and submit signatures ordinarily owe signers no guarantee of confidentiality. For persons with the "civic courage" to participate in this process, the State's decision to make accessible what they voluntarily place in the public sphere should not deter them from engaging in the expressive act of petition signing. Disclosure of the identity of petition signers, moreover, in no way directly impairs the ability of anyone to speak and associate for political ends either publicly or privately.

Given the relative weight of the interests at stake and the traditionally public nature of initiative and referendum processes, the Court rightly rejects petitioners' constitutional challenge to the State of Washington's petition disclosure regulations. These same considerations also mean that any party attempting to challenge particular applications of the State's regulations will bear a heavy burden. Even when a referendum involves a particularly controversial subject and some petition signers fear harassment from nonstate actors, a State's important interests in "protect[ing] the integrity and reliability of the initiative process" remain undiminished, and the State retains significant discretion in advancing those interests. Likewise, because the expressive interests implicated by the act of petition signing are always modest, I find it difficult to see how any incremental disincentive to sign a petition would tip the constitutional balance. Case-specific relief may be available when a State selectively applies a facially neutral petition disclosure rule in a manner that discriminates based on the content of referenda or the viewpoint of petition signers, or in the rare circumstance in which disclosure poses a reasonable probability of serious and widespread harassment that the State is unwilling or unable to control. Allowing case-specific invalidation under a more forgiving standard would unduly diminish the substantial breathing room States are afforded to adopt and implement reasonable, nondiscriminatory measures like the disclosure requirement now at issue. Accordingly, courts presented with an as-applied challenge to a regulation authorizing the disclosure of referendum petitions should be deeply skeptical of any assertion that the Constitution, which embraces political transparency, compels States to conceal the identity of persons who seek to participate in lawmaking through a state-created referendum process. With this understanding, I join the opinion of the Court.

Justice STEVENS, with whom Justice BREYER joins, concurring in part and concurring in the judgment.

This is not a hard case. It is not about a restriction on voting or on speech and does not involve a classic disclosure requirement. Rather, the case concerns a neutral, nondiscriminatory policy of disclosing information already in the State's possession that, it has been alleged, might one day indirectly burden petition signatories. The burden imposed by Washington's application of the Public Records Act (PRA) to referendum petitions in the vast majority, if not all, its applications is not substantial. And the State has given a more than adequate justification for its choice.

For a number of reasons, the application of the PRA to referendum petitions does not substantially burden any individual's expression. First, it is not "a regulation of pure speech." It does not prohibit expression, nor does it require that any person signing a petition disclose or say anything at all. Nor does the State's disclosure alter the content of a speaker's message.

Second, any effect on speech that disclosure might have is minimal. The PRA does not necessarily make it more difficult to circulate or obtain signatures on a petition, or to communicate one's views generally. Regardless of whether someone signs a referendum petition, that person remains free to say anything to anyone at any time. If disclosure indirectly burdens a speaker, "the amount of speech covered" is small— only a single, narrow message conveying one fact in one place. And while the democratic act of casting a ballot or signing a petition does serve an expressive purpose, the act does not involve any "interactive communication," and is "not principally" a method of "individual expression of political sentiment."

Weighed against the possible burden on constitutional rights are the State's justifications for its rule. In this case, the State has posited a perfectly adequate justification: an interest in deterring and detecting petition fraud. Given the pedigree of this interest and of similar regulations, the State need not produce concrete evidence that the PRA is the best way to prevent fraud.

There remains the issue of petitioners' as-applied challenge. As a matter of law, the Court is correct to keep open the possibility that in particular instances in which a policy such as the PRA burdens expression "by the public enmity attending publicity," speakers may have a winning constitutional claim. "'[F]rom time to time throughout history,'" persecuted groups have been able "'to criticize oppressive practices and laws either anonymously or not at all.'"

In my view, this is unlikely to occur in cases involving the PRA. Any burden on speech that petitioners posit is speculative as well as indirect. For an as-applied challenge to a law such as the PRA to succeed, there would have to be a significant threat of harassment directed at those who sign the petition that cannot be mitigated by law enforcement measures. Moreover, the character of the law challenged in a referendum does not, in itself, affect the analysis. Debates about tax policy and regulation of private property can become just as heated as debates about domestic partnerships. And as a general matter, it is very difficult to show that by later disclosing the names of petition signatories, individuals will be less willing to sign petitions. Just as we have in the past, I would demand strong evidence before concluding that an indirect and speculative chain of events imposes a substantial burden on speech. A statute "is not to be upset upon hypothetical and unreal possibilities, if it would be good upon the facts as they are."

Justice SCALIA, concurring in the judgment.

Plaintiffs claim the First Amendment, as applied to the States through the Fourteenth Amendment, forbids the State of Washington to release to the public signed referendum petitions, which they submitted to the State in order to suspend operation of a law and put it to a popular vote. I doubt whether signing a petition that has the effect of suspending a law fits within "the freedom of speech" at all. But even if, as the Court concludes, it does, a long history of practice shows that the First Amendment does not prohibit public disclosure.

We should not repeat and extend the mistake of *McIntyre v. Ohio Elections Comm'n* (1995). There, with neither textual support nor precedents requiring the result, the Court invalidated a form of election regulation that had been widely used by the States since the end of the 19th century. The Court held that an Ohio statute prohibiting the distribution of anonymous campaign literature violated the First and Fourteenth Amendments.

Today's opinion acknowledges such a right, finding that it can be denied here only because of the State's interest in "preserving the integrity of the electoral process." In my view this is not a matter for judicial interest-balancing. Our Nation's longstanding traditions of legislating and voting in public refute the claim that the First Amendment accords a right to anonymity in the performance of an act with governmental effect. "A governmental practice that has become general throughout the United States, and particularly one that has the validation of long, accepted usage, bears a strong presumption of constitutionality."

When a Washington voter signs a referendum petition subject to the PRA, he is acting as a legislator. The Washington Constitution vests "[t]he legislative authority" of the State in the legislature, but "the people reserve to themselves the power . . . to approve or reject at the polls any act, item, section, or part of any bill, act, or law passed by the legislature."

Plaintiffs point to no precedent from this Court holding that legislating is protected by the First Amendment. Nor do they identify historical evidence demonstrating that "the freedom of speech" the First Amendment codified encompassed a right to legislate without public disclosure. This should come as no surprise; the exercise of lawmaking power in the United States has traditionally been public.

Legislating was not the only governmental act that was public in America. Voting was public until 1888 when the States began to adopt the Australian secret ballot. We have acknowledged the existence of a First Amendment interest in voting, but we have never said that it includes the right to vote anonymously. The history of voting in the United States completely undermines that claim.

The long history of public legislating and voting contradicts plaintiffs' claim that disclosure of petition signatures having legislative effect violates the First Amendment. Just as the century-old practice of States' prohibiting anonymous electioneering was sufficient for me to reject the First Amendment claim to anonymity in *McIntyre,* the many-centuries-old practices of public legislating and voting are sufficient for me to reject plaintiffs' claim.

Plaintiffs raise concerns that the disclosure of petition signatures may lead to threats and intimidation. Of course nothing prevents the people of Washington from keeping petition signatures secret to avoid that—just as nothing prevented the States from moving to the secret ballot. But there is no constitutional basis for this Court to impose that course upon the States-or to insist (as today's opinion does) that it can only be avoided by the demonstration of a "sufficiently important governmental interest." And it may even be a bad idea to keep petition signatures secret. There are laws against threats and intimidation; and harsh criticism, short of unlawful action, is a price our people have traditionally been willing to pay for self-governance. Requiring people to stand up in public for their political acts fosters civic courage, without which democracy is doomed. For my part, I do not look forward to a society which, thanks to the Supreme Court, campaigns anonymously *(McIntyre)* and even exercises the direct democracy of initiative and referendum hidden from public scrutiny and protected from the accountability of criticism. This does not resemble the Home of the Brave.

Justice THOMAS, dissenting.

Just as "[c]onfidence in the integrity of our electoral processes is essential to the functioning of our participatory democracy," so too is citizen *participation* in those processes, which necessarily entails political speech and association under the First Amendment. In my view, compelled disclosure of signed referendum and initiative petitions under the Washington Public Records Act (PRA), severely burdens those rights and chills citizen participation in the referendum process. Given those burdens, I would hold that Washington's decision to subject all referendum petitions to public disclosure is unconstitutional because there will always be a less restrictive means by which Washington can vindicate its stated interest in preserving the integrity of its referendum process. I respectfully dissent.

Washington's construction of the PRA "on its face impose[s] a severe burden," compelled disclosure of privacy in political association protected by the First Amendment, on all referendum signers. Accordingly, I would consider petitioners' facial challenge here. For purposes of this case, I will assume that to prevail, petitioners must satisfy our most rigorous standard, and show that there is "'no set of circumstances . . . under which the'" PRA could be constitutionally applied to a referendum or initiative petition, "*i.e.,* that the [PRA] is unconstitutional in all of its applications."

This Court has long recognized the "vital relationship between" political association "and privacy in one's associations," and held that "[t]he Constitution protects against the compelled disclosure of political associations and beliefs." This constitutional protection "yield[s] only to a subordinating interest of the State that is compelling, and then only if there is a substantial relation between the information sought and an overriding and compelling state interest." Thus, unlike the Court, I read our precedents to require application of strict scrutiny to laws that compel disclosure of protected First Amendment association. Under that standard, a disclosure requirement passes constitutional muster only if it is narrowly tailored—*i.e.,* the least restrictive means-to serve a compelling state interest.

Washington's application of the PRA to a referendum petition does not survive strict scrutiny.

Washington first contends that it has a compelling interest in "transparency and accountability," which it claims encompasses several subordinate interests: preserving the integrity of its election process, preventing corruption, deterring fraud, and correcting mistakes by the secretary of state or by petition signers.

I am not persuaded that Washington's interest in protecting the integrity and reliability of its referendum process, as the State has defined that interest, is compelling. But I need not answer that question here. Even assuming the interest is compelling, on-demand disclosure of a referendum petition to any person under the PRA is "a blunderbuss approach" to furthering that interest, not the least restrictive means of doing so.

There is no apparent reason why Washington must broadly disclose referendum signers' names and addresses in this manner to vindicate the interest that it invokes here. Washington—which is in possession of that information because of referendum regulations that petitioners do not challenge—could put the names and addresses of referendum signers into a similar electronic database that state employees could search *without* subjecting the name and address of each signer to wholesale public disclosure.

The secretary could electronically cross-reference the referendum database against the "statewide voter registration list" contained in Washington's "statewide voter registration database," to ensure that each referendum signer meets Washington's residency and voter registration requirements. Doing so presumably would drastically reduce or eliminate possible errors or mistakes that Washington argues the secretary *might* make, since it would allow the secretary to verify virtually all of the signatures instead of the mere "3 to 5%" he "ordinarily checks."

Washington admits that creating this sort of electronic referendum database "could be done." Implementing such a system would not place a heavy burden on Washington; "the Secretary of State's staff" already uses an "electronic voter registration database" in its "verification process."

It is readily apparent that Washington can vindicate its stated interest in "transparency and accountability" through a number of more narrowly tailored means than wholesale public disclosure. Accordingly, this interest cannot justify applying the PRA to a referendum petition.

The Court is asked to assess the constitutionality of the PRA only with regard to referendum petitions. The question before us is whether *all* signers of *all* referendum petitions must resort to "substantial litigation over an extended time," to prevent Washington from trenching on their protected First Amendment rights by subjecting their referendum-petition signatures to on-demand public disclosure. In my view, they need not.

C. Types of Unprotected and Less Protected Speech

1. Incitement of illegal activity (casebook, p. 1322)

Although it did not concern incitement, in *Holder v. Humanitarian Law Project* (2010), the Court upheld a federal law which makes a crime to "materially assist" foreign terrorist organizations. Many of the same considerations as in the incitement cases were evident in the opinions of the justices.

HOLDER v. HUMANITARIAN LAW PROJECT
130 S.Ct. _____ (2010)

Chief Justice ROBERTS delivered the opinion of the Court.

Congress has prohibited the provision of "material support or resources" to certain foreign organizations that engage in terrorist activity.

18 U.S.C. § 2339B(a)(1). That prohibition is based on a finding that the specified organizations "are so tainted by their criminal conduct that any contribution to such an organization facilitates that conduct." The plaintiffs in this litigation seek to provide support to two such organizations. Plaintiffs claim that they seek to facilitate only the lawful, nonviolent purposes of those groups, and that applying the material-support law to prevent them from doing so violates the Constitution. In particular, they claim that the statute is too vague, in violation of the Fifth Amendment, and that it infringes their rights to freedom of speech and association, in violation of the First Amendment. We conclude that the material-support statute is constitutional as applied to the particular activities plaintiffs have told us they wish to pursue. We do not, however, address the resolution of more difficult cases that may arise under the statute in the future.

I

This litigation concerns 18 U.S.C. § 2339B, which makes it a federal crime to "knowingly provid[e] material support or resources to a foreign terrorist organization." Congress has amended the definition of "material support or resources" periodically, but at present it is defined as follows: "[T]he term 'material support or resources' means any property, tangible or intangible, or service, including currency or monetary instruments or financial securities, financial services, lodging, training, expert advice or assistance, safehouses, false documentation or identification, communications equipment, facilities, weapons, lethal substances, explosives, personnel (1 or more individuals who may be or include oneself), and transportation, except medicine or religious materials."

The authority to designate an entity a "foreign terrorist organization" rests with the Secretary of State. She may, in consultation with the Secretary of the Treasury and the Attorney General, so designate an organization upon finding that it is foreign, engages in "terrorist activity" or "terrorism," and thereby "threatens the security of United States nationals or the national security of the United States." "'[N]ational security' means the national defense, foreign relations, or economic interests of the United States." § 1189(d)(2). An entity designated a foreign terrorist organization may seek review of that designation before the D.C. Circuit within 30 days of that designation.

In 1997, the Secretary of State designated 30 groups as foreign terrorist organizations. Two of those groups are the Kurdistan Workers' Party (also known as the Partiya Karkeran Kurdistan, or PKK) and the Liberation Tigers of Tamil Eelam (LTTE). The PKK is an organization founded in 1974 with the aim of establishing an independent Kurdish state in southeastern Turkey. The LTTE is an organization founded in 1976 for the purpose of creating an independent Tamil state in Sri Lanka. The District Court in this action found that the PKK and the LTTE engage in political and humanitarian activities. The Government has presented evidence that both groups have also committed numerous terrorist attacks, some of which have harmed American citizens. The LTTE sought judicial review of its designation as a foreign terrorist organization; the D.C. Circuit upheld that designation. The PKK did not challenge its designation.

Plaintiffs in this litigation are two U.S. citizens and six domestic organizations.

II

Given the complicated 12-year history of this litigation, we pause to clarify the questions before us. Plaintiffs challenge § 2339B's prohibition on four types of material support-"training," "expert advice or assistance," "service," and "personnel." They raise three constitutional claims. First, plaintiffs claim that § 2339B violates the Due Process Clause of the Fifth Amendment because these four statutory terms are impermissibly vague. Second, plaintiffs claim that § 2339B violates their freedom of speech under the First Amendment. Third, plaintiffs claim that § 2339B violates their First Amendment freedom of association.

Plaintiffs do not challenge the above statutory terms in all their applications. Rather, plaintiffs claim that § 2339B is invalid to the extent it prohibits them from engaging in certain specified activities. With respect to the HLP, those activities are: (1) "train[ing] members of [the] PKK on how to use humanitarian and international law to peacefully resolve disputes"; (2) "engag[ing] in political advocacy on behalf of Kurds who live in Turkey"; and (3) "teach[ing] PKK members how to petition various representative bodies such as the United Nations for relief." With respect to the other plaintiffs, those activities are: (1) "train[ing] members of [the] LTTE to present claims for tsunami-related aid to mediators and international bodies"; (2) "offer[ing] their legal expertise in negotiating peace agreements between the LTTE and the Sri Lankan government"; and (3) "engag[ing] in political advocacy on behalf of Tamils who live in Sri Lanka."

III

Plaintiffs claim, as a threshold matter, that we should affirm the Court of Appeals without reaching any issues of constitutional law. They contend that we should interpret the material-support statute, when applied to speech, to require proof that a defendant intended to further a foreign terrorist organization's illegal activities. That interpretation, they say, would end the litigation because plaintiffs' proposed activities consist of speech, but plaintiffs do not intend to further unlawful conduct by the PKK or the LTTE.

We reject plaintiffs' interpretation of § 2339B because it is inconsistent with the text of the statute. Section 2339B(a)(1) prohibits "knowingly" providing material support. It then specifically describes the type of knowledge that is required: "To violate this paragraph, a person must have knowledge that the organization is a designated terrorist organization . . . , that the organization has engaged or engages in terrorist activity . . . , or that the organization has engaged or engages in terrorism. . . . " Congress plainly spoke to the necessary mental state for a violation of § 2339B, and it chose knowledge about the organization's connection to terrorism, not specific intent to further the organization's terrorist activities.

Scales v. United States (1961) is the case on which plaintiffs most heavily rely, but it is readily distinguishable. That case involved the Smith Act, which prohibited membership in a group advocating the violent overthrow of the government. The Court held that a person could not be convicted under the statute unless he had knowledge of the group's illegal advocacy and a specific intent to bring about violent overthrow. This action is different: Section 2339B does not criminalize mere membership in a designated foreign terrorist organization. It instead prohibits providing "material support" to such a group. Nothing about *Scales* suggests the need for a specific intent requirement in such a case.

IV

We turn to the question whether the material-support statute, as applied to plaintiffs, is impermissibly vague under the Due Process Clause of the Fifth Amendment. "A conviction fails to comport with due process if the statute under which it is obtained fails to provide a person of ordinary intelligence fair notice of what is prohibited, or is so standardless that it authorizes or encourages seriously discriminatory enforcement."

As a general matter, the statutory terms at issue here are quite different from the sorts of terms that we have previously declared to be vague. We have in the past "struck down statutes that tied criminal culpability to whether the defendant's conduct was 'annoying' or 'indecent'—wholly subjective judgments without statutory definitions, narrowing context, or settled legal meanings." Applying the statutory terms in this action— "training," "expert advice or assistance," "service," and "personnel"—does not require similarly untethered, subjective judgments.

Congress also took care to add narrowing definitions to the material-support statute over time. These definitions increased the clarity of the statute's terms. See § 2339A(b)(2) ("'training' means instruction or teaching designed to impart a specific skill, as opposed to general knowledge"); § 2339A(b)(3) ("'expert advice or assistance' means advice or assistance derived from scientific, technical or other specialized knowledge"); § 2339B(h) (clarifying the scope of "personnel"). And the knowledge requirement of the statute further reduces any potential for vagueness, as we have held with respect to other statutes containing a similar requirement.

Of course, the scope of the material-support statute may not be clear in every application. But the dispositive point here is that the statutory terms are clear in their application to plaintiffs' proposed conduct, which means that plaintiffs' vagueness challenge must fail. Even assuming that a heightened standard applies because the material-support statute potentially implicates speech, the statutory terms are not vague as applied to plaintiffs.

Most of the activities in which plaintiffs seek to engage readily fall within the scope of the terms "training" and "expert advice or assistance." Plaintiffs want to "train members of [the] PKK on how to use humanitarian and international law to peacefully resolve disputes," and "teach PKK members how to petition various representative bodies such as the United Nations for relief." A person of ordinary intelligence would understand that instruction on resolving disputes through international law falls within the statute's definition of "training" because it imparts a "specific skill," not "general knowledge." Plaintiffs' activities also fall comfortably within the scope of "expert advice or assistance": A reasonable person would recognize that teaching the PKK how to petition for humanitarian relief before the United Nations involves advice derived from, as the statute puts it, "specialized knowledge." In fact, plaintiffs themselves have repeatedly used the terms "training" and "expert advice" throughout this litigation to describe their own proposed activities, demonstrating that these common terms readily and naturally cover plaintiffs' conduct.

As for "personnel," Congress enacted a limiting definition in IRTPA that answers plaintiffs' vagueness concerns. Providing material support that constitutes "personnel" is defined as knowingly providing a person "to work under that terrorist organization's direction or control or to organize, manage, supervise, or otherwise direct the operation of that organization." The statute makes clear that "personnel" does not cover *independent* advocacy: "Individuals who act entirely independently of the foreign terrorist organization to advance its goals or objectives shall not be considered to be working under the foreign terrorist organization's direction and control."

"[S]ervice" similarly refers to concerted activity, not independent advocacy. Context confirms that ordinary meaning here. The statute prohibits providing a service "*to* a foreign terrorist organization." The use of the word "to" indicates a connection between the service and the foreign group. We think a person of ordinary intelligence would understand that independently advocating for a cause is different from providing a service to a group that is advocating for that cause.

V

A

We next consider whether the material-support statute, as applied to plaintiffs, violates the freedom of speech guaranteed by the First Amendment. Both plaintiffs and the Government take extreme positions on this question. Plaintiffs claim that Congress has banned their "pure political speech." It has not. Under the material-support statute, plaintiffs may say anything they wish on any topic. They may speak and write freely about the PKK and LTTE, the governments of Turkey and Sri Lanka, human rights, and international law. They may advocate before the United Nations. As the Government states: "The statute does not prohibit independent advocacy or expression of any kind." Section 2339B also "does not prevent [plaintiffs] from becoming members of the PKK and LTTE or impose any sanction on them for doing so." Congress has not, therefore, sought to suppress ideas or opinions in the form of "pure political speech." Rather, Congress has prohibited "material support," which most often does not take the form of speech at all. And when it does, the statute is carefully drawn to cover only a narrow category of speech to, under the direction of, or in coordination with foreign groups that the speaker knows to be terrorist organizations.

For its part, the Government takes the foregoing too far, claiming that the only thing truly at issue in this litigation is conduct, not speech. Section 2339B is directed at the fact of plaintiffs' interaction with the PKK and LTTE, the Government contends, and only incidentally burdens their expression. The Government is wrong that the only thing actually at issue in this litigation is conduct, and therefore wrong to argue that [intermediate scrutiny is] the correct standard of review. § 2339B regulates speech on the basis of its content. Plaintiffs want to speak to the PKK and the LTTE, and whether they may do so under § 2339B depends on what they say. If plaintiffs' speech to those groups imparts a "specific skill" or communicates advice derived from "specialized knowledge"—for example, training on the use of international law or advice on petitioning the United Nations—then it is barred. On the other hand, plaintiffs' speech is not barred if it imparts only general or unspecialized knowledge.

B

The First Amendment issue before us is more refined than either plaintiffs or the Government would have it. It is not whether the Government may prohibit pure political speech, or may prohibit material support in the form of conduct. It is instead whether the Government may prohibit what plaintiffs want to do—provide material support to the PKK and LTTE in the form of speech.

Everyone agrees that the Government's interest in combating terrorism is an urgent objective of the highest order. The objective of combating terrorism does not justify prohibiting their speech, plaintiffs argue, because their support will advance only the legitimate activities of the designated terrorist organizations, not their terrorism.

Whether foreign terrorist organizations meaningfully segregate support of their legitimate activities from support of terrorism is an empirical question. When it enacted § 2339B in 1996, Congress made specific findings regarding the serious threat posed by international terrorism. One of those findings explicitly rejects plaintiffs' contention that their support would not further the terrorist activities of the PKK and LTTE: "[F]oreign organizations that engage in terrorist activity are so tainted by their criminal conduct that *any contribution to such an organization* facilitates that conduct."

Plaintiffs argue that the reference to "any contribution" in this finding meant only monetary support. There is no reason to read the finding to be so limited, particularly because Congress expressly prohibited so much more than monetary support in § 2339B. Congress's use of the term "contribution" is best read to reflect a determination that any form of material support furnished "to" a foreign terrorist organization should be barred, which is precisely what the material-support statute does.

The PKK and the LTTE are deadly groups. "The PKK's insurgency has claimed more than 22,000 lives." The LTTE has engaged in extensive suicide bombings and political assassinations, including killings of the Sri Lankan President, Security Minister, and Deputy Defense Minister. "On January 31, 1996, the LTTE exploded a truck bomb filled with an estimated 1,000 pounds of explosives at the Central Bank in Colombo, killing 100 people and injuring more than 1,400. This bombing was the most deadly terrorist incident in the world in 1996." It is not difficult to conclude as Congress did that the "tain[t]" of such violent activities is so great that working in coordination with or at the command of the PKK and LTTE serves to legitimize and further their terrorist means.

Material support meant to "promot[e] peaceable, lawful conduct," can further terrorism by foreign groups in multiple ways. "Material support" is a valuable resource by definition. Such support frees up other resources within the organization that may be put to violent ends. It also importantly helps lend legitimacy to foreign terrorist groups—legitimacy that makes it easier for those groups to persist, to recruit members, and to raise funds—all of which facilitate more terrorist attacks. "Terrorist organizations do not maintain *organizational* 'firewalls' that would prevent or deter . . . sharing and commingling of support and benefits." "[I]nvestigators have revealed how terrorist groups systematically conceal their activities behind charitable, social, and political fronts." "Indeed, some designated foreign terrorist organizations use social and political components to recruit personnel to carry out terrorist operations, and to provide support to criminal terrorists and their families in aid of such operations."

Money is fungible, and "[w]hen foreign terrorist organizations that have a dual structure raise funds, they highlight the civilian and humanitarian ends to which such moneys could be put." But "there is reason to believe that foreign terrorist organizations do not maintain legitimate *financial* firewalls between those funds raised for civil, nonviolent activities, and those ultimately used to support violent, terrorist operations." Thus, "[f]unds raised ostensibly for charitable purposes have in the past been redirected by some terrorist groups to fund the purchase of arms and explosives."

The dissent argues that there is "no natural stopping place" for the proposition that aiding a foreign terrorist organization's lawful activity promotes the terrorist organization as a whole. But Congress has settled on just such a natural stopping place: The statute reaches only material support coordinated with or under the direction of a designated foreign terrorist organization. Independent advocacy that might be viewed as promoting the group's legitimacy is not covered.

Providing foreign terrorist groups with material support in any form also furthers terrorism by straining the United States' relationships with its allies and undermining cooperative efforts between nations to prevent terrorist attacks. We see no reason to question Congress's finding that "international cooperation is required for an effective response to terrorism, as demonstrated by the numerous multilateral conventions in force providing universal prosecutive jurisdiction over persons involved in a variety of terrorist acts, including hostage taking, murder of an internationally protected person, and aircraft piracy and sabotage." The material-support statute furthers this international effort by prohibiting aid for foreign terrorist groups that harm the United States' partners abroad.

C

In analyzing whether it is possible in practice to distinguish material support for a foreign terrorist group's violent activities and its nonviolent activities, we do not rely exclusively on our own inferences drawn from the record evidence. We have before us an affidavit stating the Executive Branch's conclusion on that question. The State Department informs us that "[t]he experience and analysis of the U.S. government agencies charged with combating terrorism strongly suppor[t]" Congress's finding that all contributions to foreign terrorist organizations further their terrorism.

That evaluation of the facts by the Executive, like Congress's assessment, is entitled to deference. This litigation implicates sensitive and weighty interests of national security and foreign affairs. The PKK and the LTTE have committed terrorist acts against American citizens abroad, and the material-support statute addresses acute foreign policy concerns involving relationships with our Nation's allies.

Our precedents, old and new, make clear that concerns of national security and foreign relations do not warrant abdication of the judicial role. We do not defer to the Government's reading of the First Amendment, even when such interests are at stake. But when it comes to collecting evidence and drawing factual inferences in this area, "the lack of competence on the part of the courts is marked," and respect for the Government's conclusions is appropriate.

At bottom, plaintiffs simply disagree with the considered judgment of Congress and the Executive that providing material support to a designated foreign terrorist organization—even seemingly benign support—bolsters the terrorist activities of that organization. That judgment, however, is entitled to significant weight, and we have persuasive evidence before us to sustain it. Given the sensitive interests in national security and foreign affairs at stake, the political branches have adequately substantiated their determination that, to serve the Government's interest in preventing terrorism, it was necessary to prohibit providing material support in the form of training, expert advice, personnel, and services to foreign terrorist groups, even if the supporters meant to promote only the groups' nonviolent ends.

We turn to the particular speech plaintiffs propose to undertake. First, plaintiffs propose to "train members of [the] PKK on how to use humanitarian and international law to peacefully resolve disputes." Congress can, consistent with the First Amendment, prohibit this direct training. It is wholly foreseeable that the PKK could use the "specific skill[s]" that plaintiffs propose to impart, as part of a broader strategy to promote terrorism. The PKK could, for example, pursue peaceful negotiation as a means of buying time to recover from short-term setbacks, lulling opponents into complacency, and ultimately preparing for renewed attacks. A foreign terrorist organization introduced to the structures of the international legal system might use the information to threaten, manipulate, and disrupt. This possibility is real, not remote.

Second, plaintiffs propose to "teach PKK members how to petition various representative bodies such as the United Nations for relief." The Government acts within First Amendment strictures in banning this proposed speech because it teaches the organization how to acquire "relief," which plaintiffs never define with any specificity, and which could readily include monetary aid. Indeed, earlier in this litigation, plaintiffs sought to teach the LTTE "to present claims for tsunami-related aid to mediators and international bodies," which naturally included monetary relief. Money is fungible and Congress logically concluded that money a terrorist group such as the PKK obtains using the techniques plaintiffs propose to teach could be redirected to funding the group's violent activities.

Finally, plaintiffs propose to "engage in political advocacy on behalf of Kurds who live in Turkey," and "engage in political advocacy on behalf of Tamils who live in Sri Lanka." As explained above, plaintiffs do not specify their expected level of coordination with the PKK or LTTE or suggest what exactly their "advocacy" would consist of. Plaintiffs' proposals are phrased at such a high level of generality that they cannot prevail in this preenforcement challenge.

All this is not to say that any future applications of the material-support statute to speech or advocacy will survive First Amendment scrutiny. It is also not to say that any other statute relating to speech and terrorism would satisfy the First Amendment. In particular, we in no way suggest that a regulation of independent speech would pass constitutional muster, even if the Government were to show that such speech benefits foreign terrorist organizations. We also do not suggest that Congress could extend the same prohibition on material support at issue here to domestic organizations. We simply hold that, in prohibiting the particular forms of support that plaintiffs seek to provide to foreign terrorist groups, § 2339B does not violate the freedom of speech.

VI

Plaintiffs' final claim is that the material-support statute violates their freedom of association under the First Amendment. Plaintiffs argue that the statute criminalizes the mere fact of their associating with the PKK and the LTTE. The Court of Appeals correctly rejected this claim because the statute does not penalize mere association with a foreign terrorist organization. As the Ninth Circuit put it: "The statute does not prohibit being a member of one of the designated groups or vigorously promoting and supporting the political goals of the group. . . . What [§ 2339B] prohibits is the act of giving material support. . . . " Plaintiffs want to do the latter. Our decisions scrutinizing penalties on simple association or assembly are therefore inapposite.

* * *

The Preamble to the Constitution proclaims that the people of the United States ordained and established that charter of government in part to "provide for the common defence." As Madison explained, "[s]ecurity against foreign danger is . . . an avowed and essential object of the American Union." We hold that, in regulating the particular forms of support that plaintiffs seek to provide to foreign terrorist organizations, Congress has pursued that objective consistent with the limitations of the First and Fifth Amendments.

Justice BREYER, with whom Justices GINSBURG, and SOTOMAYOR join, dissenting.

Like the Court, and substantially for the reasons it gives, I do not think this statute is unconstitutionally vague. But I cannot agree with the Court's conclusion that the Constitution permits the Government to prosecute the plaintiffs criminally for engaging in coordinated teaching and advocacy furthering the designated organizations' lawful political objectives. In my view, the Government has not met its burden of showing that an interpretation of the statute that would prohibit this speech- and association-related activity serves the Government's compelling interest in combating terrorism. And I would interpret the statute as normally placing activity of this kind outside its scope.

The plaintiffs, all United States citizens or associations, now seek an injunction and declaration providing that, without violating the statute, they can (1) "train members of [the] PKK on how to use humanitarian and international law to peacefully resolve disputes"; (2) "engage in political advocacy on behalf of Kurds who live in Turkey"; (3) "teach PKK members how to petition various representative bodies such as the United Nations for relief"; and (4) "engage in political advocacy on behalf of Tamils who live in Sri Lanka." All these activities are of a kind that the First Amendment ordinarily protects.

In my view, the Government has not made the strong showing necessary to justify under the First Amendment the criminal prosecution of those who engage in these activities. All the activities involve the communication and advocacy of political ideas and lawful means of achieving political ends. Even the subjects the plaintiffs wish to teach—using international law to resolve disputes peacefully or petitioning the United Nations, for instance—concern political speech. We cannot avoid the constitutional significance of these facts on the basis that some of this speech takes place outside the United States and is directed at foreign governments, for the activities also involve advocacy in *this* country directed to *our* government and *its* policies. The plaintiffs, for example, wish to write and distribute publications and to speak before the United States Congress.

That this speech and association for political purposes is the *kind* of activity to which the First Amendment ordinarily offers its strongest protection is elementary. Although in the Court's view the statute applies only where the PKK helps to coordinate a defendant's activities, the simple fact of "coordination" alone cannot readily remove protection that the First Amendment would otherwise grant. That amendment, after all, also protects the freedom of association. "Coordination" with a political group, like membership, involves association.

"Coordination" with a group that engages in unlawful activity also does not deprive the plaintiffs of the First Amendment's protection under any traditional "categorical" exception to its protection. The plaintiffs do not propose to solicit a crime. They will not engage in fraud or defamation or circulate obscenity. And the First Amendment protects advocacy even of *unlawful* action so long as that advocacy is not "directed to inciting or producing *imminent lawless action* and . . . *likely to incite or produce* such action." Here the plaintiffs seek to advocate peaceful, *lawful* action to secure *political* ends; and they seek to teach others how to do the same. No one contends that the plaintiffs' speech to these organizations can be prohibited as incitement. Moreover, the Court has previously held that a person who associates with a group that uses unlawful means to achieve its ends does not thereby necessarily forfeit the First Amendment's protection for freedom of association.

Not even the "serious and deadly problem" of international terrorism can require *automatic* forfeiture of First Amendment rights. After all, this Court has recognized that not "'[e]ven the war power . . . remove[s] constitutional limitations safeguarding essential liberties.'" Thus, there is no general First Amendment exception that applies here. If the statute is constitutional in this context, it would have to come with a strong justification attached.

The Government does identify a compelling countervailing interest, namely, the interest in protecting the security of the United States and its nationals from the threats that foreign terrorist organizations pose by denying those organizations financial and other fungible resources. I do not dispute the importance of this interest. But I do dispute whether the interest can justify the statute's criminal prohibition. To put the matter more specifically, precisely how does application of the statute to the protected activities before us *help achieve* that important security-related end?

The Government makes two efforts to answer this question. *First,* the Government says that the plaintiffs' support for these organizations is "fungible" in the same sense as other forms of banned support. Being fungible, the plaintiffs' support could, for example, free up other resources, which the organization might put to terrorist ends. The pro-position that the two very different kinds of "support" are "fungible," however, is not *obviously* true. There is no *obvious* way in which under-taking advocacy for political change through peaceful means or teaching the PKK and LTTE, say, how to petition the United Nations for political change is fungible with other resources that might be put to more sinister ends in the way that donations of money, food, or computer training are fungible. It is far from obvious that these advocacy activities can them-selves be redirected, or will free other resources that can be directed, towards terrorist ends.

Second, the Government says that the plaintiffs' proposed activities will "bolste[r] a terrorist organization's efficacy and strength in a com-munity" and "undermin[e] this nation's efforts to *delegitimize and weaken* those groups." In the Court's view, too, the Constitution permits application of the statute to activities of the kind at issue in part because those activities could provide a group that engages in terrorism with "legitimacy." The Court suggests that, armed with this greater "legiti-macy," these organizations will more readily be able to obtain material support of the kinds Congress plainly intended to ban—money, arms, lodging, and the like.

Yet the Government does not claim that the statute forbids *any* speech "legitimating" a terrorist group. Rather, it reads the statute as permitting (1) membership in terrorist organizations, (2) "peaceably assembling with members of the PKK and LTTE for lawful discussion," or (3) "independent advocacy" on behalf of these organizations. The Court, too, emphasizes that activities not "*coordinated with*" the terrorist groups are not banned.

But this "legitimacy" justification cannot by itself warrant suppression of political speech, advocacy, and association. Speech, association, and related activities on behalf of a group will often, perhaps always, help to legitimate that group. Thus, were the law to accept a "legitimating" effect, in and of itself and without qualification, as providing sufficient grounds for imposing such a ban, the First Amendment battle would be lost in untold instances where it should be won. Once one accepts this argument, there is no natural stopping place.

Nor can the Government overcome these considerations simply by narrowing the covered activities to those that involve *coordinated,* rather than *independent,* advocacy. Conversations, discussions, or logistical arrangements might well prove necessary to carry out the speech-related activities here at issue (just as conversations and discussions are a necessary part of *membership* in any organization). The Government does not distinguish this kind of "coordination" from any other. I am not aware of any form of words that might be used to describe "coordination" that would not, at a minimum, seriously chill not only the kind of activities the plaintiffs raise before us, but also the "independent advocacy" the Government purports to permit. And, as for the Government's willingness to distinguish *independent* advocacy from *coordinated* advocacy, the former is *more* likely, not *less* likely, to confer legitimacy than the latter. Thus, other things being equal, the distinction "coordination" makes is arbitrary in respect to furthering the statute's purposes. And a rule of law that finds the "legitimacy" argument adequate in respect to the latter would have a hard time distinguishing a statute that sought to attack the former.

Throughout, the majority emphasizes that it would defer strongly to Congress' "informed judgment." But here, there is no evidence that Congress has made such a judgment regarding the specific activities at issue in these cases. I concede that the Government's expertise in foreign affairs may warrant deference in respect to many matters, *e.g.,* our relations with Turkey. But it remains for this Court to decide whether the Government has shown that such an interest justifies criminalizing speech activity otherwise protected by the First Amendment. And the fact that other nations may like us less for granting that protection cannot in and of itself carry the day.

For the reasons I have set forth, I believe application of the statute as the Government interprets it would gravely and without adequate justification injure interests of the kind the First Amendment protects. Thus, there is "a serious doubt" as to the statute's constitutionality. And where that is so, we must "ascertain whether a construction of the statute is fairly possible by which the question may be avoided."

I believe that a construction that would avoid the constitutional problem is "fairly possible." In particular, I would read the statute as criminalizing First-Amendment-protected pure speech and association only when the defendant knows or intends that those activities will assist the organization's unlawful terrorist actions. Under this reading, the Government would have to show, at a minimum, that such defendants provided support that they knew was significantly likely to help the organization pursue its unlawful terrorist aims.

This reading of the statute protects those who engage in pure speech and association ordinarily protected by the First Amendment. But it does not protect that activity where a defendant purposefully intends it to help terrorism or where a defendant knows (or willfully blinds himself to the fact) that the activity is significantly likely to assist terrorism. Where the activity fits into these categories of purposefully or knowingly supporting terrorist ends, the act of providing material support to a known terrorist organization bears a close enough relation to terrorist acts that, in my view, it likely can be prohibited notwithstanding any First Amendment interest. At the same time, this reading does not require the Government to undertake the difficult task of proving which, as between peaceful and nonpeaceful purposes, a defendant specifically preferred; knowledge is enough. This reading is consistent with the statute's text. The statute prohibits "*knowingly* provid[ing] *material* support or resources to a foreign terrorist organization."

Having interpreted the statute to impose the *mens rea* requirement just described, I would remand the cases so that the lower courts could consider more specifically the precise activities in which the plaintiffs still wish to engage and determine whether and to what extent a grant of declaratory and injunctive relief were warranted.

In sum, these cases require us to consider how to apply the First Amendment where national security interests are at stake. When deciding such cases, courts are aware and must respect the fact that the Constitution entrusts to the Executive and Legislative Branches the power to provide for the national defense, and that it grants particular authority to the

President in matters of foreign affairs. Nonetheless, this Court has also made clear that authority and expertise in these matters do not automatically trump the Court's own obligation to secure the protection that the Constitution grants to individuals. In these cases, for the reasons I have stated, I believe the Court has failed to examine the Government's justifications with sufficient care. It has failed to insist upon specific evidence, rather than general assertion. It has failed to require tailoring of means to fit compelling ends. And ultimately it deprives the individuals before us of the protection that the First Amendment demands.

3. Sexually Oriented Speech

i. The Broadcast Media (casebook, p. 1412)

In *FCC v. Pacifica Foundation* (casebook, p. 1412), the Supreme Court held that television and radio broadcasters could be punished for indecent speech. The Court did not deal, though, with a single use of a profanity (the so-called 'fleeting expletive'). In 2004, the Federal Communication Commission changed its policy so that it would punish single uses of profanities. The United States Court of Appeals for the Second Circuit invalidated this, concluding that it was an arbitrary agency action in violation of the Administrative Procedures Act. The Supreme Court reversed in a 5-4 decision. Justice Scalia's majority opinion focused entirely on the Administrative Procedures Act and did not decide the First Amendment question.

6. Conduct that communicates

c. When may the government regulate conduct that communicates?

vi. Is corporate spending protected speech? (casebook, p. 1257)

In *McConnell v. Federal Election Commission* (2003), the Court upheld a federal law that prohibited the ability of corporations and unions to spend money for broadcast advertisements for or against an identifiable candidate 30 days before a primary or 60 days before a general election. In *Citizens United v. Federal Election Commission* (2010), the Court overruled this aspect of *McConnell* and held that corporations and unions have the right to spend as much as they choose in independent expenditures. The Court did not consider the constitutionality of restrictions on corporate and union contributions to candidates.

CITIZENS UNITED v. FEDERAL ELECTION COMMISSION
130 S.Ct. 876 (2010)

Justice KENNEDY delivered the opinion of the Court.

Federal law prohibits corporations and unions from using their general treasury funds to make independent expenditures for speech defined as an "electioneering communication" or for speech expressly advocating the election or defeat of a candidate. Limits on electioneering communications were upheld in *McConnell v. Federal Election Comm'n* (2003). The holding of *McConnell* rested to a large extent on an earlier case, *Austin v. Michigan Chamber of Commerce* (1990). *Austin* had held that political speech may be banned based on the speaker's corporate identity.

In this case we are asked to reconsider *Austin* and, in effect, *McConnell*. It has been noted that "*Austin* was a significant departure from ancient First Amendment principles." We agree with that conclusion and hold that *stare decisis* does not compel the continued acceptance of *Austin*. The Government may regulate corporate political speech through disclaimer and disclosure requirements, but it may not suppress that speech altogether. We turn to the case now before us.

I

Citizens United is a nonprofit corporation. Citizens United has an annual budget of about $12 million. Most of its funds are from donations by individuals; but, in addition, it accepts a small portion of its funds from for-profit corporations.

In January 2008, Citizens United released a film entitled *Hillary: The Movie*. It is a 90-minute documentary about then-Senator Hillary Clinton, who was a candidate in the Democratic Party's 2008 Presidential primary elections. *Hillary* mentions Senator Clinton by name and depicts interviews with political commentators and other persons, most of them quite critical of Senator Clinton. *Hillary* was released in theaters and on DVD, but Citizens United wanted to increase distribution by making it available through video-on-demand.

Video-on-demand allows digital cable subscribers to select programming from various menus, including movies, television shows, sports, news, and music. The viewer can watch the program at any time and can elect to rewind or pause the program. In December 2007, a cable company offered, for a payment of $1.2 million, to make *Hillary* available on a video-on-demand channel called "Elections '08." Some video-on-demand services require viewers to pay a small fee to view a selected program, but here the proposal was to make *Hillary* available to viewers free of charge.

To implement the proposal, Citizens United was prepared to pay for the video-on-demand; and to promote the film, it produced two 10-second ads and one 30-second ad for *Hillary*. Each ad includes a short (and, in our view, pejorative) statement about Senator Clinton, followed by the name of the movie and the movie's Website address. Citizens United desired to promote the video-on-demand offering by running advertisements on broadcast and cable television.

Before the Bipartisan Campaign Reform Act of 2002 (BCRA), federal law prohibited—and still does prohibit—corporations and unions from using general treasury funds to make direct contributions to candidates or independent expenditures that expressly advocate the election or defeat of a candidate, through any form of media, in connection with certain qualified federal elections. BCRA § 203 amended § 441b to prohibit any "electioneering communication" as well. An electioneering communication is defined as "any broadcast, cable, or satellite communication" that "refers to a clearly identified candidate for Federal office" and is made within 30 days of a primary or 60 days of a general election. The Federal Election Commission's (FEC) regulations further define an electioneering communication as a communication that is "publicly distributed." Corporations and unions are barred from using their general treasury funds for express advocacy or electioneering communications. They may establish, however, a "separate segregated fund" (known as a political action committee, or PAC) for these purposes. The moneys received by the segregated fund are limited to donations from stockholders and employees of the corporation or, in the case of unions, members of the union.

In December 2007, Citizens United sought declaratory and injunctive relief against the FEC.

[II]

The First Amendment provides that "Congress shall make no law . . . abridging the freedom of speech." Laws enacted to control or suppress speech may operate at different points in the speech process. The following are just a few examples of restrictions that have been attempted at different stages of the speech process-all laws found to be invalid: restrictions requiring a permit at the outset, *Watchtower Bible & Tract Soc. of N.Y., Inc. v. Village of Stratton* (2002); imposing a burden by impounding proceeds on receipts or royalties, *Simon & Schuster, Inc. v. Members of N.Y. State Crime Victims Bd.*; seeking to exact a cost after the speech occurs, *New York Times Co. v. Sullivan* (1964); and subjecting the speaker to criminal penalties, *Brandenburg v. Ohio* (1969) *(per curiam)*.

The law before us is an outright ban, backed by criminal sanctions. Section 441b makes it a felony for all corporations—including nonprofit advocacy corporations—either to expressly advocate the election or defeat of candidates or to broadcast electioneering communications within 30 days of a primary election and 60 days of a general election. Thus, the following acts would all be felonies under § 441b: The Sierra Club runs an ad, within the crucial phase of 60 days before the general election, that exhorts the public to disapprove of a Congressman who favors logging in national forests; the National Rifle Association publishes a book urging the public to vote for the challenger because the incumbent U.S. Senator supports a handgun ban; and the American Civil Liberties Union creates a Web site telling the public to vote for a Presidential candidate in light of that candidate's defense of free speech. These prohibitions are classic examples of censorship.

Section 441b is a ban on corporate speech notwithstanding the fact that a PAC created by a corporation can still speak. A PAC is a separate association from the corporation. Even if a PAC could somehow allow a corporation to speak-and it does not-the option to form PACs does not alleviate the First Amendment problems with § 441b. PACs are burdensome alternatives; they are expensive to administer and subject to extensive regulations.

Section 441b's prohibition on corporate independent expenditures is thus a ban on speech. As a "restriction on the amount of money a person or group can spend on political communication during a campaign," that statute "necessarily reduces the quantity of expression by restricting the number of issues discussed, the depth of their exploration, and the size of the audience reached." *Buckley v. Valeo* (1976) *(per curiam)*. Were the Court to uphold these restrictions, the Government could repress speech by silencing certain voices at any of the various points in the speech process. If § 441b applied to individuals, no one would believe that it is merely a time, place, or manner restriction on speech. Its purpose and effect are to silence entities whose voices the Government deems to be suspect.

Speech is an essential mechanism of democracy, for it is the means to hold officials accountable to the people. The right of citizens to inquire, to hear, to speak, and to use information to reach consensus is a precondition to enlightened self-government and a necessary means to protect it. The First Amendment "'has its fullest and most urgent application' to speech uttered during a campaign for political office."

For these reasons, political speech must prevail against laws that would suppress it, whether by design or inadvertence. Laws that burden political speech are "subject to strict scrutiny," which requires the Government to prove that the restriction "furthers a compelling interest and is narrowly tailored to achieve that interest."

Premised on mistrust of governmental power, the First Amendment stands against attempts to disfavor certain subjects or viewpoints. Prohibited, too, are restrictions distinguishing among different speakers, allowing speech by some but not others. As instruments to censor, these categories are interrelated: Speech restrictions based on the identity of the speaker are all too often simply a means to control content.

Quite apart from the purpose or effect of regulating content, moreover, the Government may commit a constitutional wrong when by law it identifies certain preferred speakers. By taking the right to speak from some and giving it to others, the Government deprives the disadvantaged person or class of the right to use speech to strive to establish worth, standing, and respect for the speaker's voice. The Government may not by these means deprive the public of the right and privilege to determine for itself what speech and speakers are worthy of consideration. The First Amendment protects speech and speaker, and the ideas that flow from each.

We find no basis for the proposition that, in the context of political speech, the Government may impose restrictions on certain disfavored speakers. Both history and logic lead us to this conclusion.

A

The Court has recognized that First Amendment protection extends to corporations. This protection has been extended by explicit holdings to the context of political speech. Under the rationale of these precedents, political speech does not lose First Amendment protection "simply because its source is a corporation." The Court has thus rejected the argument that political speech of corporations or other associations should be treated differently under the First Amendment simply because such associations are not "natural persons."

Thus the law stood until *Austin*. *Austin* "uph[eld] a direct restriction on the independent expenditure of funds for political speech for the first time in [this Court's] history." There, the Michigan Chamber of Commerce sought to use general treasury funds to run a newspaper ad supporting a specific candidate. Michigan law, however, prohibited corporate independent expenditures that supported or opposed any candidate for state office. A violation of the law was punishable as a felony. The Court sustained the speech prohibition.

To bypass *Buckley* and *Bellotti*, the *Austin* Court identified a new governmental interest in limiting political speech: an antidistortion interest. *Austin* found a compelling governmental interest in preventing "the corrosive and distorting effects of immense aggregations of wealth that are accumulated with the help of the corporate form and that have little or no correlation to the public's support for the corporation's political ideas."

B

The Court is thus confronted with conflicting lines of precedent: a pre-*Austin* line that forbids restrictions on political speech based on the speaker's corporate identity and a post-*Austin* line that permits them. No case before *Austin* had held that Congress could prohibit independent expenditures for political speech based on the speaker's corporate identity. Before *Austin* Congress had enacted legislation for this purpose, and the Government urged the same proposition before this Court.

As for *Austin*'s antidistortion rationale, the Government does little to defend it. And with good reason, for the rationale cannot support § 441b. If the First Amendment has any force, it prohibits Congress from fining or jailing citizens, or associations of citizens, for simply engaging in political speech. If the antidistortion rationale were to be accepted, however, it would permit Government to ban political speech simply because the speaker is an association that has taken on the corporate form. The Government contends that *Austin* permits it to ban corporate expenditures for almost all forms of communication stemming from a corporation. If *Austin* were correct, the Government could prohibit a corporation from expressing political views in media beyond those presented here, such as by printing books. The Government responds "that the FEC has never applied this statute to a book," and if it did, "there would be quite [a] good as-applied challenge." This troubling assertion of brooding governmental power cannot be reconciled with the confidence and stability in civic discourse that the First Amendment must secure.

Political speech is "indispensable to decisionmaking in a democracy, and this is no less true because the speech comes from a corporation rather than an individual." This protection for speech is inconsistent with *Austin's* antidistortion rationale. *Austin* sought to defend the antidistortion rationale as a means to prevent corporations from obtaining "'an unfair advantage in the political marketplace'" by using "'resources amassed in the economic marketplace.'"

Either as support for its antidistortion rationale or as a further argument, the *Austin* majority undertook to distinguish wealthy individuals from corporations on the ground that "[s]tate law grants corporations special advantages-such as limited liability, perpetual life, and favorable treatment of the accumulation and distribution of assets." This does not suffice, however, to allow laws prohibiting speech. "It is rudimentary that the State cannot exact as the price of those special advantages the forfeiture of First Amendment rights."

It is irrelevant for purposes of the First Amendment that corporate funds may "have little or no correlation to the public's support for the corporation's political ideas." All speakers, including individuals and the media, use money amassed from the economic marketplace to fund their speech. The First Amendment protects the resulting speech, even if it was enabled by economic transactions with persons or entities who disagree with the speaker's ideas.

Austin's antidistortion rationale would produce the dangerous, and unacceptable, consequence that Congress could ban political speech of media corporations. Media corporations are now exempt from § 441b's ban on corporate expenditures. Yet media corporations accumulate wealth with the help of the corporate form, the largest media corporations have "immense aggregations of wealth," and the views expressed by media corporations often "have little or no correlation to the public's support" for those views. Thus, under the Government's reasoning, wealthy media corporations could have their voices diminished to put them on par with other media entities. There is no precedent for permitting this under the First Amendment.

The media exemption discloses further difficulties with the law now under consideration. There is no precedent supporting laws that attempt to distinguish between corporations which are deemed to be exempt as media corporations and those which are not. "We have consistently rejected the proposition that the institutional press has any constitutional privilege beyond that of other speakers." With the advent of the Internet and the decline of print and broadcast media, moreover, the line between the media and others who wish to comment on political and social issues becomes far more blurred.

The law's exception for media corporations is, on its own terms, all but an admission of the invalidity of the antidistortion rationale. And the exemption results in a further, separate reason for finding this law invalid: Again by its own terms, the law exempts some corporations but covers others, even though both have the need or the motive to communicate their views. The exemption applies to media corporations owned or controlled by corporations that have diverse and substantial investments and participate in endeavors other than news. So even assuming the most doubtful proposition that a news organization has a right to speak when others do not, the exemption would allow a conglomerate that owns both a media business and an unrelated business to influence or control the media in order to advance its overall business interest. At the same time, some other corporation, with an identical business interest but no media outlet in its ownership structure, would be forbidden to speak or inform the public about the same issue. This differential treatment cannot be squared with the First Amendment.

There is simply no support for the view that the First Amendment, as originally understood, would permit the suppression of political speech by media corporations. The Framers may not have anticipated modern business and media corporations. Yet television networks and major newspapers owned by media corporations have become the most important means of mass communication in modern times. The First Amendment was certainly not understood to condone the suppression of political speech in society's most salient media. It was understood as a response to the repression of speech and the press that had existed in England and the heavy taxes on the press that were imposed in the colonies.

Austin interferes with the "open marketplace" of ideas protected by the First Amendment. It permits the Government to ban the political speech of millions of associations of citizens.

The censorship we now confront is vast in its reach. The Government has "muffle[d] the voices that best represent the most significant segments of the economy." And "the electorate [has been] deprived of information, knowledge and opinion vital to its function." By suppressing the speech of manifold corporations, both for-profit and nonprofit, the Government prevents their voices and viewpoints from reaching the public and advising voters on which persons or entities are hostile to their interests.

The purpose and effect of this law is to prevent corporations, including small and nonprofit corporations, from presenting both facts and opinions to the public. When Government seeks to use its full power, including the criminal law, to command where a person may get his or her information or what distrusted source he or she may not hear, it uses censorship to control thought. This is unlawful. The First Amendment confirms the freedom to think for ourselves.

What we have said also shows the invalidity of other arguments made by the Government. For the most part relinquishing the antidistortion rationale, the Government falls back on the argument that corporate political speech can be banned in order to prevent corruption or its appearance. In *Buckley,* the Court found this interest "sufficiently important" to allow limits on contributions but did not extend that reasoning to expenditure limits. When *Buckley* examined an expenditure ban, it found "that the governmental interest in preventing corruption and the appearance of corruption [was] inadequate to justify [the ban] on independent expenditures."

A single footnote in *Bellotti* purported to leave open the possibility that corporate independent expenditures could be shown to cause corruption. For the reasons explained above, we now conclude that independent expenditures, including those made by corporations, do not give rise to corruption or the appearance of corruption.

When *Buckley* identified a sufficiently important governmental interest in preventing corruption or the appearance of corruption, that interest was limited to *quid pro quo* corruption. The fact that speakers may have influence over or access to elected officials does not mean that these officials are corrupt. The appearance of influence or access, furthermore, will not cause the electorate to lose faith in our democracy. By definition, an independent expenditure is political speech presented to the electorate that is not coordinated with a candidate. The fact that a corporation, or any other speaker, is willing to spend money to try to persuade voters presupposes that the people have the ultimate influence over elected officials.

The Government contends further that corporate independent expenditures can be limited because of its interest in protecting dissenting shareholders from being compelled to fund corporate political speech. This asserted interest, like *Austin*'s antidistortion rationale, would allow the Government to ban the political speech even of media corporations. Assume, for example, that a shareholder of a corporation that owns a newspaper disagrees with the political views the newspaper expresses. Under the Government's view, that potential disagreement could give the Government the authority to restrict the media corporation's political speech. The First Amendment does not allow that power. There is, furthermore, little evidence of abuse that cannot be corrected by shareholders "through the procedures of corporate democracy."

We need not reach the question whether the Government has a compelling interest in preventing foreign individuals or associations from influencing our Nation's political process. Section 441b is not limited to corporations or associations that were created in foreign countries or funded predominately by foreign shareholders.

C

Our precedent is to be respected unless the most convincing of reasons demonstrates that adherence to it puts us on a course that is sure error. For the reasons above, it must be concluded that *Austin* was not well reasoned. The Government defends *Austin,* relying almost entirely on "the quid pro quo interest, the corruption interest or the shareholder interest," and not *Austin*'s expressed antidistortion rationale. When neither party defends the reasoning of a precedent, the principle of adhering to that precedent through *stare decisis* is diminished.

Austin is undermined by experience since its announcement. Political speech is so ingrained in our culture that speakers find ways to circumvent campaign finance laws. Our Nation's speech dynamic is changing, and informative voices should not have to circumvent onerous restrictions to exercise their First Amendment rights. Speakers have become adept at presenting citizens with sound bites, talking points, and scripted messages that dominate the 24-hour news cycle. Corporations, like individuals, do not have monolithic views. On certain topics corporations may possess valuable expertise, leaving them the best equipped to point out errors or fallacies in speech of all sorts, including the speech of candidates and elected officials.

Due consideration leads to this conclusion: *Austin* should be and now is overruled. We return to the principle established in *Buckley* and *Bellotti* that the Government may not suppress political speech on the basis of the speaker's corporate identity. No sufficient governmental interest justifies limits on the political speech of nonprofit or for-profit corporations.

Given our conclusion we are further required to overrule the part of *McConnell* that upheld BCRA § 203's extension of § 441b's restrictions on corporate independent expenditures. The *McConnell* Court relied on the antidistortion interest recognized in *Austin* to uphold a greater restriction on speech than the restriction upheld in *Austin* and we have found this interest unconvincing and insufficient. This part of *McConnell* is now overruled.

IV

Citizens United next challenges BCRA's disclaimer and disclosure provisions as applied to *Hillary* and the three advertisements for the movie. Under BCRA § 311, televised electioneering communications funded by anyone other than a candidate must include a disclaimer that "'____ is responsible for the content of this advertising.'" The required statement must be made in a "clearly spoken manner," and displayed on the screen in a "clearly readable manner" for at least four seconds. It must state that the communication "is not authorized by any candidate or candidate's committee"; it must also display the name and address (or Web site address) of the person or group that funded the advertisement. Under BCRA § 201, any person who spends more than $10,000 on electioneering communications within a calendar year must file a disclosure statement with the FEC. That statement must identify the person making the expenditure, the amount of the expenditure, the election to which the communication was directed, and the names of certain contributors.

Disclaimer and disclosure requirements may burden the ability to speak, but they "impose no ceiling on campaign-related activities," and "do not prevent anyone from speaking." The Court has subjected these requirements to "exacting scrutiny," which requires a "substantial relation" between the disclosure requirement and a "sufficiently important" governmental interest.

In *Buckley,* the Court explained that disclosure could be justified based on a governmental interest in "provid[ing] the electorate with information" about the sources of election-related spending.

For the reasons stated below, we find the statute valid as applied to the ads for the movie and to the movie itself. The First Amendment protects political speech; and disclosure permits citizens and shareholders to react to the speech of corporate entities in a proper way. This transparency enables the electorate to make informed decisions and give proper weight to different speakers and messages.

We find no constitutional impediment to the application of BCRA's disclaimer and disclosure requirements to a movie broadcast via video-on-demand. And there has been no showing that, as applied in this case, these requirements would impose a chill on speech or expression.

V

When word concerning the plot of the movie *Mr. Smith Goes to Washington* reached the circles of Government, some officials sought, by persuasion, to discourage its distribution. Under *Austin,* though, officials could have done more than discourage its distribution-they could have banned the film. After all, it, like *Hillary*, was speech funded by a corporation that was critical of Members of Congress. *Mr. Smith Goes to Washington* may be fiction and caricature; but fiction and caricature can be a powerful force.

Some members of the public might consider *Hillary* to be insightful and instructive; some might find it to be neither high art nor a fair discussion on how to set the Nation's course; still others simply might suspend judgment on these points but decide to think more about issues and candidates. Those choices and assessments, however, are not for the Government to make. "The First Amendment underwrites the freedom to experiment and to create in the realm of thought and speech. Citizens must be free to use new forms, and new forums, for the expression of ideas. The civic discourse belongs to the people, and the Government may not prescribe the means used to conduct it."

Justice SCALIA, with whom Justice ALITO joins, and with whom Justice THOMAS joins in part, concurring.

I join the opinion of the Court. I write separately to address JUSTICE STEVENS' discussion of "*Original Understandings.*" This section of the dissent purports to show that today's decision is not supported by the original understanding of the First Amendment. The dissent attempts this demonstration, however, in splendid isolation from the text of the First Amendment. It never shows why "the freedom of speech" that was the right of Englishmen did not include the freedom to speak in association with other individuals, including association in the corporate form. To be sure, in 1791 (as now) corporations could pursue only the objectives set forth in their charters; but the dissent provides no evidence that their speech in the pursuit of those objectives could be censored.

Instead of taking this straightforward approach to determining the Amendment's meaning, the dissent embarks on a detailed exploration of the Framers' views about the "role of corporations in society." The Framers didn't like corporations, the dissent concludes, and therefore it follows (as night the day) that corporations had no rights of free speech. Of course the Framers' personal affection or disaffection for corporations is relevant only insofar as it can be thought to be reflected in the understood meaning of the text they enacted—not, as the dissent suggests, as a freestanding substitute for that text. But the dissent's distortion of proper analysis is even worse than that. Though faced with a constitutional text that makes no distinction between types of speakers, the dissent feels no necessity to provide even an isolated statement from the founding era to the effect that corporations are *not* covered, but places the burden on petitioners to bring forward statements showing that they *are*.

Despite the corporation-hating quotations the dissent has dredged up, it is far from clear that by the end of the 18th century corporations were despised. If so, how came there to be so many of them? The dissent's statement that there were few business corporations during the eighteenth century—"only a few hundred during all of the 18th century"—is misleading. There were approximately 335 charters issued to business corporations in the United States by the end of the 18th century.

Even if we thought it proper to apply the dissent's approach of excluding from First Amendment coverage what the Founders disliked, and even if we agreed that the Founders disliked founding-era corporations; modern corporations might not qualify for exclusion. Most of the Founders' resentment towards corporations was directed at the state-granted monopoly privileges that individually chartered corporations enjoyed. Modern corporations do not have such privileges, and would probably have been favored by most of our enterprising Founders—excluding, perhaps, Thomas Jefferson and others favoring perpetuation of an agrarian society. Moreover, if the Founders' specific intent with respect to corporations is what matters, why does the dissent ignore the Founders' views about other legal entities that have more in common with modern business corporations than the founding-era corporations? At the time of the founding, religious, educational, and literary corporations were incorporated under general incorporation statutes, much as business corporations are today. Were all of these silently excluded from the protections of the First Amendment?

The lack of a textual exception for speech by corporations cannot be explained on the ground that such organizations did not exist or did not speak. To the contrary, colleges, towns and cities, religious institutions, and guilds had long been organized as corporations at common law and under the King's charter, and as I have discussed, the practice of incorporation only expanded in the United States. Both corporations and voluntary associations actively petitioned the Government and expressed their views in newspapers and pamphlets.

Historical evidence relating to the textually similar clause "the freedom of . . . the press" also provides no support for the proposition that the First Amendment excludes conduct of artificial legal entities from the scope of its protection. The freedom of "the press" was widely understood to protect the publishing activities of individual editors and printers. But these individuals often acted through newspapers, which (much like corporations) had their own names, outlived the individuals who had founded them, could be bought and sold, were sometimes owned by more than one person, and were operated for profit. Their activities were not stripped of First Amendment protection simply because they were carried out under the banner of an artificial legal entity. And the notion which follows from the dissent's view, that modern newspapers, since they are incorporated, have free-speech rights only at the sufferance of Congress, boggles the mind.

In passing, the dissent also claims that the Court's conception of corruption is unhistorical. The Framers "would have been appalled," it says, by the evidence of corruption in the congressional findings supporting the Bipartisan Campaign Reform Act of 2002. For this proposition, the dissent cites a law review article arguing that "corruption" was originally understood to include "moral decay" and even actions taken by citizens in pursuit of private rather than public ends. It is hard to see how this has anything to do with what sort of corruption can be combated by restrictions on political speech. Moreover, if speech can be prohibited because, in the view of the Government, it leads to "moral decay" or does not serve "public ends," then there is no limit to the Government's censorship power.

The dissent says that when the Framers "constitutionalized the right to free speech in the First Amendment, it was the free speech of individual Americans that they had in mind." That is no doubt true. All the provisions of the Bill of Rights set forth the rights of individual men and women-not, for example, of trees or polar bears. But the individual person's right to speak includes the right to speak *in association with other individual persons.* Surely the dissent does not believe that speech by the Republican Party or the Democratic Party can be censored because it is not the speech of "an individual American." It is the speech of many individual Americans, who have associated in a common cause, giving the leadership of the party the right to speak on their behalf. The association of individuals in a business corporation is no different—or at least it cannot be denied the right to speak on the simplistic ground that it is not "an individual American."

But to return to, and summarize, my principal point, which is the conformity of today's opinion with the original meaning of the First Amendment. The Amendment is written in terms of "speech," not speakers. Its text offers no foothold for excluding any category of speaker, from single individuals to partnerships of individuals, to unincorporated associations of individuals, to incorporated associations of individuals—and the dissent offers no evidence about the original meaning of the text to support any such exclusion. We are therefore simply left with the question whether the speech at issue in this case is "speech" covered by the First Amendment. No one says otherwise. A documentary film critical of a potential Presidential candidate is core political speech, and its nature as such does not change simply because it was funded by a corporation. Nor does the character of that funding produce any reduction whatever in the "inherent worth of the speech" and "its capacity for informing the public," *First Nat. Bank of Boston v. Bellotti* (1978). Indeed, to exclude or impede corporate speech is to muzzle the principal agents of the modern free economy. We should celebrate rather than condemn the addition of this speech to the public debate

Justice STEVENS, with whom Justice GINSBURG, Justice BREYER, and Justice SOTOMAYOR join, concurring in part and dissenting in part.

The real issue in this case concerns how, not if, the appellant may finance its electioneering. Citizens United is a wealthy nonprofit corporation that runs a political action committee (PAC) with millions of dollars in assets. Under the Bipartisan Campaign Reform Act of 2002 (BCRA), it could have used those assets to televise and promote *Hillary: The Movie* wherever and whenever it wanted to. It also could have spent unrestricted sums to broadcast *Hillary* at any time other than the 30 days before the last primary election. Neither Citizens United's nor any other corporation's speech has been "banned." All that the parties dispute is whether Citizens United had a right to use the funds in its general treasury to pay for broadcasts during the 30-day period. The notion that the First Amendment dictates an affirmative answer to that question is, in my judgment, profoundly misguided. Even more misguided is the notion that the Court must rewrite the law relating to campaign expenditures by *for-profit* corporations and unions to decide this case.

The basic premise underlying the Court's ruling is its iteration, and constant reiteration, of the proposition that the First Amendment bars regulatory distinctions based on a speaker's identity, including its "identity" as a corporation. While that glittering generality has rhetorical appeal, it is not a correct statement of the law. Nor does it tell us when a corporation may engage in electioneering that some of its shareholders oppose. It does not even resolve the specific question whether Citizens United may be required to finance some of its messages with the money in its PAC. The conceit that corporations must be treated identically to natural persons in the political sphere is not only inaccurate but also inadequate to justify the Court's disposition of this case.

In the context of election to public office, the distinction between corporate and human speakers is significant. Although they make enormous contributions to our society, corporations are not actually members of it. They cannot vote or run for office. Because they may be managed and controlled by nonresidents, their interests may conflict in fundamental respects with the interests of eligible voters. The financial resources, legal structure, and instrumental orientation of corporations raise legitimate concerns about their role in the electoral process. Our lawmakers have a compelling constitutional basis, if not also a democratic duty, to take measures designed to guard against the potentially deleterious effects of corporate spending in local and national races.

The majority's approach to corporate electioneering marks a dramatic break from our past. Congress has placed special limitations on campaign spending by corporations ever since the passage of the Tillman Act in 1907. We have unanimously concluded that this "reflects a permissible assessment of the dangers posed by those entities to the electoral process," *FEC v. National Right to Work Comm.* (1982) *(NRWC),* and have accepted the "legislative judgment that the special characteristics of the corporate structure require particularly careful regulation." The Court today rejects a century of history when it treats the distinction between corporate and individual campaign spending as an invidious novelty born of *Austin v. Michigan Chamber of Commerce* (1990). Relying largely on individual dissenting opinions, the majority blazes through our precedents, overruling or disavowing a body of case law.

Although I concur in the Court's decision to sustain BCRA's disclosure provisions and join Part IV of its opinion, I emphatically dissent from its principal holding.

I

The Court's ruling threatens to undermine the integrity of elected institutions across the Nation. The path it has taken to reach its outcome will, I fear, do damage to this institution. Before turning to the question whether to overrule *Austin* and part of *McConnell,* it is important to explain why the Court should not be deciding that question. [Justice STEVENS then argued that the case should have been decided as an "as applied" rather than a facial challenge and also that it should have been decided on narrower grounds.]

II

The final principle of judicial process that the majority violates is the most transparent: *stare decisis.* I am not an absolutist when it comes to *stare decisis,* in the campaign finance area or in any other. No one is. But if this principle is to do any meaningful work in supporting the rule of law, it must at least demand a significant justification, beyond the preferences of five Justices, for overturning settled doctrine. "[A] decision to overrule should rest on some special reason over and above the belief that a prior case was wrongly decided." *Planned Parenthood of Southeastern Pa. v. Casey* (1992). No such justification exists in this case, and to the contrary there are powerful prudential reasons to keep faith with our precedents.

The Court's central argument for why *stare decisis* ought to be trumped is that it does not like *Austin*. The opinion "was not well reasoned," our colleagues assert, and it conflicts with First Amendment principles. This, of course, is the Court's merits argument, the many defects in which we will soon consider. I am perfectly willing to concede that if one of our precedents were dead wrong in its reasoning or irreconcilable with the rest of our doctrine, there would be a compelling basis for revisiting it. But neither is true of *Austin,* and restating a merits argument with additional vigor does not give it extra weight in the *stare decisis* calculus.

We have recognized that "*[s]tare decisis* has special force when legislators or citizens 'have acted in reliance on a previous decision, for in this instance overruling the decision would dislodge settled rights and expectations or require an extensive legislative response.'" *Stare decisis* protects not only personal rights involving property or contract but also the ability of the elected branches to shape their laws in an effective and coherent fashion. Today's decision takes away a power that we have long permitted these branches to exercise. State legislatures have relied on their authority to regulate corporate electioneering, confirmed in *Austin,* for more than a century. The Federal Congress has relied on this authority for a comparable stretch of time, and it specifically relied on *Austin* throughout the years it spent developing and debating BCRA. The total record it compiled was *100,000 pages* long. Pulling out the rug beneath Congress after affirming the constitutionality of § 203 six years ago shows great disrespect for a coequal branch.

In the end, the Court's rejection of *Austin* and *McConnell* comes down to nothing more than its disagreement with their results. Virtually every one of its arguments was made and rejected in those cases, and the majority opinion is essentially an amalgamation of resuscitated dissents. The only relevant thing that has changed since *Austin* and *McConnell* is the composition of this Court. Today's ruling thus strikes at the vitals of *stare decisis,* "the means by which we ensure that the law will not merely change erratically, but will develop in a principled and intelligible fashion" that "permits society to presume that bedrock principles are founded in the law rather than in the proclivities of individuals."

III

The novelty of the Court's procedural dereliction and its approach to *stare decisis* is matched by the novelty of its ruling on the merits. The ruling rests on several premises. First, the Court claims that *Austin* and *McConnell* have "banned" corporate speech. Second, it claims that the First Amendment precludes regulatory distinctions based on speaker identity, including the speaker's identity as a corporation. Third, it claims that *Austin* and *McConnell* were radical outliers in our First Amendment tradition and our campaign finance jurisprudence. Each of these claims is wrong.

The So-Called "Ban"

Pervading the Court's analysis is the ominous image of a "categorical ba[n]" on corporate speech. Indeed, the majority invokes the specter of a "ban" on nearly every page of its opinion. This characterization is highly misleading, and needs to be corrected.

In fact it already has been. Our cases have repeatedly pointed out that, "[c]ontrary to the [majority's] critical assumptions," the statutes upheld in *Austin* and *McConnell* do "not impose an *absolute* ban on all forms of corporate political spending." For starters, both statutes provide exemptions for PACs, separate segregated funds established by a corporation for political purposes. "The ability to form and administer separate segregated funds," we observed in *McConnell*, "has provided corporations and unions with a constitutionally sufficient opportunity to engage in express advocacy. That has been this Court's unanimous view."

Under BCRA, any corporation's "stockholders and their families and its executive or administrative personnel and their families" can pool their resources to finance electioneering communications. A significant and growing number of corporations avail themselves of this option; during the most recent election cycle, corporate and union PACs raised nearly a billion dollars. Administering a PAC entails some administrative burden, but so does complying with the disclaimer, disclosure, and reporting requirements that the Court today upholds, and no one has suggested that the burden is severe for a sophisticated for-profit corporation. To the extent the majority is worried about this issue, it is important to keep in mind that we have no record to show how substantial the burden really is, just the majority's own unsupported factfinding. Like all other natural persons, every shareholder of every corporation remains entirely free under *Austin* and *McConnell* to do however much electioneering she pleases outside of the corporate form. The owners of a "mom & pop" store can simply place ads in their own names, rather than the store's.

So let us be clear: Neither *Austin* nor *McConnell* held or implied that corporations may be silenced; the FEC is not a "censor"; and in the years since these cases were decided, corporations have continued to play a major role in the national dialogue. Laws such as § 203 target a class of communications that is especially likely to corrupt the political process, that is at least one degree removed from the views of individual citizens, and that may not even reflect the views of those who pay for it. Such laws burden political speech, and that is always a serious matter, demanding careful scrutiny. But the majority's incessant talk of a "ban" aims at a straw man.

Identity-Based Distinctions

The second pillar of the Court's opinion is its assertion that "the Government cannot restrict political speech based on the speaker's . . . identity." The case on which it relies for this proposition is *First Nat. Bank of Boston v. Bellotti* (1978). As I shall explain, the holding in that case was far narrower than the Court implies.

[I]n a variety of contexts, we have held that speech can be regulated differentially on account of the speaker's identity, when identity is understood in categorical or institutional terms. The Government routinely places special restrictions on the speech rights of students, prisoners, members of the Armed Forces, foreigners, and its own employees. When such restrictions are justified by a legitimate governmental interest, they do not necessarily raise constitutional problems. In contrast to the blanket rule that the majority espouses, our cases recognize that the Government's interests may be more or less compelling with respect to different classes of speakers, and that the constitutional rights of certain categories of speakers, in certain contexts, "'are not automatically coextensive with the rights'" that are normally accorded to members of our society.

The election context is distinctive in many ways, and the Court, of course, is right that the First Amendment closely guards political speech. But in this context, too, the authority of legislatures to enact viewpoint-neutral regulations based on content and identity is well settled. We have, for example, allowed state-run broadcasters to exclude independent candidates from televised debates. *Arkansas Ed. Television Comm'n v.*

Forbes (1998). We have upheld statutes that prohibit the distribution or display of campaign materials near a polling place. *Burson v. Freeman,* (1992). Although we have not reviewed them directly, we have never cast doubt on laws that place special restrictions on campaign spending by foreign nationals. And we have consistently approved laws that bar Government employees, but not others, from contributing to or participating in political activities.

The same logic applies to this case with additional force because it is the identity of corporations, rather than individuals, that the Legislature has taken into account. As we have unanimously observed, legislatures are entitled to decide "that the special characteristics of the corporate structure require particularly careful regulation" in an electoral context. Not only has the distinctive potential of corporations to corrupt the electoral process long been recognized, but within the area of campaign finance, corporate spending is also "furthest from the core of political expression, since corporations' First Amendment speech and association interests are derived largely from those of their members and of the public in receiving information," Campaign finance distinctions based on corporate identity tend to be less worrisome, in other words, because the "speakers" are not natural persons, much less members of our political community, and the governmental interests are of the highest order. Furthermore, when corporations, as a class, are distinguished from noncorporations, as a class, there is a lesser risk that regulatory distinctions will reflect invidious discrimination or political favoritism.

If taken seriously, our colleagues' assumption that the identity of a speaker has *no* relevance to the Government's ability to regulate political speech would lead to some remarkable conclusions. Such an assumption would have accorded the propaganda broadcasts to our troops by "Tokyo Rose" during World War II the same protection as speech by Allied commanders. More pertinently, it would appear to afford the same protection to multinational corporations controlled by foreigners as to individual Americans. Under the majority's view, I suppose it may be a First Amendment problem that corporations are not permitted to vote, given that voting is, among other things, a form of speech.

Our First Amendment Tradition

A third fulcrum of the Court's opinion is the idea that *Austin* and *McConnell* are radical outliers, "aberration[s]," in our First Amendment tradition. The Court has it exactly backwards. It is today's holding that is the radical departure from what had been settled First Amendment law. To see why, it is useful to take a long view.

Let us start from the beginning. The Court invokes "ancient First Amendment principles," and original understandings, to defend today's ruling, yet it makes only a perfunctory attempt to ground its analysis in the principles or understandings of those who drafted and ratified the Amendment. Perhaps this is because there is not a scintilla of evidence to support the notion that anyone believed it would preclude regulatory distinctions based on the corporate form. To the extent that the Framers' views are discernible and relevant to the disposition of this case, they would appear to cut strongly against the majority's position.

This is not only because the Framers and their contemporaries conceived of speech more narrowly than we now think of it, but also because they held very different views about the nature of the First Amendment right and the role of corporations in society. Those few corporations that existed at the founding were authorized by grant of a special legislative charter. The individualized charter mode of incorporation reflected the "cloud of disfavor under which corporations labored" in the early years of this Nation.

The Framers thus took it as a given that corporations could be comprehensively regulated in the service of the public welfare. Unlike our colleagues, they had little trouble distinguishing corporations from human beings, and when they constitutionalized the right to free speech in the First Amendment, it was the free speech of individual Americans that they had in mind. While individuals might join together to exercise their speech rights, business corporations, at least, were plainly not seen as facilitating such associational or expressive ends. In light of these background practices and understandings, it seems to me implausible that the Framers believed "the freedom of speech" would extend equally to all corporate speakers, much less that it would preclude legislatures from taking limited measures to guard against corporate capture of elections.

A century of more recent history puts to rest any notion that today's ruling is faithful to our First Amendment tradition. At the federal level, the express distinction between corporate and individual political spending on elections stretches back to 1907, when Congress passed the Tillman Act, banning all corporate contributions to candidates.

In sum, over the course of the past century Congress has demonstrated a recurrent need to regulate corporate participation in candidate elections to " '[p]reserv[e] the integrity of the electoral process, preven[t] corruption, . . . sustai[n] the active, alert responsibility of the individual citizen,'" protect the expressive interests of shareholders, and "'[p] reserv [e] . . . the individual citizen's confidence in government.'" Time and again, we have recognized these realities in approving measures that Congress and the States have taken. None of the cases the majority cites is to the contrary. The only thing new about *Austin* was the dissent, with its stunning failure to appreciate the legitimacy of interests recognized in the name of democratic integrity since the days of the Progressives.

IV

Having explained why this is not an appropriate case in which to revisit *Austin* and *McConnell* and why these decisions sit perfectly well with "First Amendment principles," I come at last to the interests that are at stake. The majority recognizes that *Austin* and *McConnell* may be defended on anticorruption, antidistortion, and shareholder protection rationales. It badly errs both in explaining the nature of these rationales, which overlap and complement each other, and in applying them to the case at hand.

The Anticorruption Interest

Undergirding the majority's approach to the merits is the claim that the only "sufficiently important governmental interest in preventing corruption or the appearance of corruption" is one that is "limited to *quid pro quo* corruption." While it is true that we have not always spoken about corruption in a clear or consistent voice, the approach taken by the majority cannot be right, in my judgment. It disregards our constitutional history and the fundamental demands of a democratic society.

On numerous occasions we have recognized Congress' legitimate interest in preventing the money that is spent on elections from exerting an "'undue influence on an officeholder's judgment'" and from creating "'the appearance of such influence,'" beyond the sphere of *quid pro quo* relationships. Corruption can take many forms. Bribery may be the paradigm case. But the difference between selling a vote and selling access is a matter of degree, not kind. And selling access is not qualitatively different from giving special preference to those who spent money on one's behalf. Corruption operates along a spectrum, and the majority's apparent belief that *quid pro quo* arrangements can be neatly demarcated from other improper influences does not accord with the theory or reality of politics. It certainly does not accord with the record Congress developed in passing BCRA, a record that stands as a remarkable testament to the energy and ingenuity with which corporations, unions, lobbyists, and politicians may go about scratching each other's backs—and which amply supported Congress' determination to target a limited set of especially destructive practices.

The cluster of interrelated interests threatened by such undue influence and its appearance has been well captured under the rubric of "democratic integrity." This value has underlined a century of state and federal efforts to regulate the role of corporations in the electoral process.

Antidistortion

The fact that corporations are different from human beings might seem to need no elaboration, except that the majority opinion almost completely elides it. *Austin* set forth some of the basic differences. Unlike natural persons, corporations have "limited liability" for their owners and managers, "perpetual life," separation of ownership and control, "and favorable treatment of the accumulation and distribution of assets . . . that enhance their ability to attract capital and to deploy their resources in ways that maximize the return on their shareholders' investments." Unlike voters in U.S. elections, corporations may be foreign controlled. Unlike other interest groups, business corporations have been "effectively delegated responsibility for ensuring society's economic welfare"; they inescapably structure the life of every citizen. "'[T]he resources in the treasury of a business corporation,'" furthermore, "'are not an indication of popular support for the corporation's political ideas.'" "'They reflect instead the economically motivated decisions of investors and customers. The availability of these resources may make a corporation a formidable political presence, even though the power of the corporation may be no reflection of the power of its ideas.'"

It might also be added that corporations have no consciences, no beliefs, no feelings, no thoughts, no desires. Corporations help structure and facilitate the activities of human beings, to be sure, and their "personhood" often serves as a useful legal fiction. But they are not themselves members of "We the People" by whom and for whom our Constitution was established.

These basic points help explain why corporate electioneering is not only more likely to impair compelling governmental interests, but also why restrictions on that electioneering are less likely to encroach upon First Amendment freedoms. One fundamental concern of the First Amendment is to "protec[t] the individual's interest in self-expression." Freedom of speech helps "make men free to develop their faculties," it respects their "dignity and choice," and it facilitates the value of "individual self-realization." Corporate speech, however, is derivative speech, speech by proxy. A regulation such as BCRA § 203 may affect the way in which individuals disseminate certain messages through the corporate form, but it does not prevent anyone from speaking in his or her own voice. "Within the realm of [campaign spending] generally," corporate spending is "furthest from the core of political expression."

None of this is to suggest that corporations can or should be denied an opportunity to participate in election campaigns or in any other public forum (much less that a work of art such as *Mr. Smith Goes to Washington* may be banned), or to deny that some corporate speech may contribute significantly to public debate. What it shows, however, is that *Austin*'s "concern about corporate domination of the political process," reflects more than a concern to protect governmental interests outside of the First Amendment. It also reflects a concern to *facilitate* First Amendment values by preserving some breathing room around the electoral "marketplace" of ideas, the marketplace in which the actual people of this Nation determine how they will govern themselves. The majority seems oblivious to the simple truth that laws such as § 203 do not merely pit the anticorruption interest against the First Amendment, but also pit competing First Amendment values against each other. There are, to be sure, serious concerns with any effort to balance the First Amendment rights of speakers against the First Amendment rights of listeners. But when the speakers in question are not real people and when the appeal to "First Amendment principles" depends almost entirely on the listeners' perspective, it becomes necessary to consider how listeners will actually be affected.

In critiquing *Austin*'s antidistortion rationale and campaign finance regulation more generally, our colleagues place tremendous weight on the example of media corporations. Yet it is not at all clear that *Austin* would permit § 203 to be applied to them. The press plays a unique role not only in the text, history, and structure of the First Amendment but also in facilitating public discourse; as the *Austin* Court explained, "media corporations differ significantly from other corporations in that their resources are devoted to the collection of information and its dissemination to the public." Our colleagues have raised some interesting and difficult questions about Congress' authority to regulate electioneering by the press, and about how to define what constitutes the press. *But that is not the case before us.* Section 203 does not apply to media corporations, and even if it did, Citizens United is not a media corporation. There would be absolutely no reason to consider the issue of media corporations if the majority did not, first, transform Citizens United's as-applied challenge into a facial challenge and, second, invent the theory that legislatures must eschew all "identity"-based distinctions and treat a local nonprofit news outlet exactly the same as General Motors.

Shareholder Protection

There is yet another way in which laws such as § 203 can serve First Amendment values. Interwoven with *Austin*'s concern to protect the integrity of the electoral process is a concern to protect the rights of shareholders from a kind of coerced speech: electioneering expenditures that do not "reflec [t] [their] support." When corporations use general treasury funds to praise or attack a particular candidate for office, it is the shareholders, as the residual claimants, who are effectively footing the bill. Those shareholders who disagree with the corporation's electoral message may find their financial investments being used to undermine their political convictions.

The PAC mechanism, by contrast, helps assure that those who pay for an electioneering communication actually support its content and that managers do not use general treasuries to advance personal agendas. It "'allows corporate political participation without the temptation to use corporate funds for political influence, quite possibly at odds with the sentiments of some shareholders or members.'"

V

In a democratic society, the longstanding consensus on the need to limit corporate campaign spending should outweigh the wooden application of judge-made rules. The majority's rejection of this principle "elevate[s] corporations to a level of deference which has not been seen at least since the days when substantive due process was regularly used to invalidate regulatory legislation thought to unfairly impinge upon established economic interests." At bottom, the Court's opinion is thus a rejection of the common sense of the American people, who have recognized a need to prevent corporations from undermining self-government since the founding, and who have fought against the distinctive corrupting potential of corporate electioneering since the days of Theodore Roosevelt. It is a strange time to repudiate that common sense. While American democracy is imperfect, few outside the majority of this Court would have thought its flaws included a dearth of corporate money in politics.

Justice THOMAS, concurring in part and dissenting in part.

I join all but Part IV of the Court's opinion. I dissent from Part IV of the Court's opinion, however, because the Court's constitutional analysis does not go far enough. The disclosure, disclaimer, and reporting requirements in BCRA §§ 201 and 311 are also unconstitutional.

Congress may not abridge the "right to anonymous speech" based on the "'simple interest in providing voters with additional relevant information.'" In continuing to hold otherwise, the Court misapprehends the import of "recent events" that some *amici* describe "in which donors to certain causes were blacklisted, threatened, or otherwise targeted for retaliation." The Court properly recognizes these events as "cause for concern," but fails to acknowledge their constitutional significance.

These instances of retaliation sufficiently demonstrate why this Court should invalidate mandatory disclosure and reporting requirements. But *amici* present evidence of yet another reason to do so—the threat of retaliation from *elected officials*. For example, a candidate challenging an incumbent state attorney general reported that some members of the State's business community feared donating to his campaign because they did not want to cross the incumbent; in his words, "'I go to so many people and hear the same thing: "I sure hope you beat [the incumbent], but I can't afford to have my name on your records. He might come after me next." The incumbent won reelection in 2008.

My point is not to express any view on the merits of the political controversies I describe. Rather, it is to demonstrate—using real-world, recent examples—the fallacy in the Court's conclusion that "[d]isclaimer and disclosure requirements . . . impose no ceiling on campaign-related activities, and do not prevent anyone from speaking." Of course they do. Disclaimer and disclosure requirements enable private citizens and elected officials to implement political strategies *specifically calculated* to curtail campaign-related activity and prevent the lawful, peaceful exercise of First Amendment rights.

I cannot endorse a view of the First Amendment that subjects citizens of this Nation to death threats, ruined careers, damaged or defaced property, or pre-emptive and threatening warning letters as the price for engaging in "core political speech, the 'primary object of First Amendment protection.'" Accordingly, I respectfully dissent from the Court's judgment upholding BCRA §§ 201 and 311.

E. Freedom of Association

4. Laws prohibiting discrimination (casebook, p. 1612)

In *Christian Legal Society v. Martinez* (2010), the Court upheld the constitutionality of a law school at a public university requiring student groups to accept all members and denying recognition to student groups that discriminated based on religion and sexual orientation. Notice how the majority opinion, by Justice Ginsburg, and the dissent, by Justice Alito, use very different analytical approaches and come to very different conclusions as to how to balance the competing interests of equality and freedom of association.

CHRISTIAN LEGAL SOC. CHAPTER OF THE UNIVERSITY OF CALIFORNIA, *HASTINGS COLLEGE* OF THE LAW v. MARTINEZ
130 S.Ct. _____ (2010)

Justice GINSBURG delivered the opinion of the Court.

In a series of decisions, this Court has emphasized that the First Amendment generally precludes public universities from denying student organizations access to school-sponsored forums because of the groups' viewpoints. This case concerns a novel question regarding student activities at public universities: May a public law school condition its official recognition of a student group—and the attendant use of school funds and facilities—on the organization's agreement to open eligibility for membership and leadership to all students?

In the view of petitioner Christian Legal Society (CLS), an accept-all-comers policy impairs its First Amendment rights to free speech, expressive association, and free exercise of religion by prompting it, on pain of relinquishing the advantages of recognition, to accept members who do not share the organization's core beliefs about religion and sexual orientation. From the perspective of respondent Hastings College of the Law (Hastings or the Law School), CLS seeks special dispensation from an across-the-board open-access requirement designed to further the reasonable educational purposes underpinning the school's student-organization program.

In accord with the District Court and the Court of Appeals, we reject CLS's First Amendment challenge. Compliance with Hastings' all-comers policy, we conclude, is a reasonable, viewpoint-neutral condition on access to the student-organization forum. In requiring CLS—in common with all other student organizations—to choose between welcoming all students and forgoing the benefits of official recognition, we hold, Hastings did not transgress constitutional limitations. CLS, it bears emphasis, seeks not parity with other organizations, but a preferential exemption from Hastings' policy. The First Amendment shields CLS against state prohibition of the organization's expressive activity,

however exclusionary that activity may be. But CLS enjoys no constitutional right to state subvention of its selectivity.

I

Through its "Registered Student Organization" (RSO) program, Hastings extends official recognition to student groups. Several benefits
attend this school-approved status. RSOs are eligible to seek financial
assistance from the Law School, which subsidizes their events using
funds from a mandatory student-activity fee imposed on all students.
RSOs may also use Law-School channels to communicate with students:
They may place announcements in a weekly Office-of-Student-Services
newsletter, advertise events on designated bulletin boards, send e-mails
using a Hastings-organization address, and participate in an annual
Student Organizations Fair designed to advance recruitment efforts. In
addition, RSOs may apply for permission to use the Law School's
facilities for meetings and office space. Finally, Hastings allows officially recognized groups to use its name and logo.

In exchange for these benefits, RSOs must abide by certain conditions.
Only a "non-commercial organization whose membership is limited to
Hastings students may become [an RSO]." A prospective RSO must
submit its bylaws to Hastings for approval, and if it intends to use the
Law School's name or logo, it must sign a license agreement. Critical
here, all RSOs must undertake to comply with Hastings' "Policies and
Regulations Applying to College Activities, Organizations and Stu-
dents."

The Law School's Policy on Nondiscrimination (Nondiscrimination
Policy), which binds RSOs, states:

"[Hastings] is committed to a policy against legally impermissible, arbitrary or
unreasonable discriminatory practices. All groups, including administration, faculty,
student governments, [Hastings]-owned student residence facilities and programs
sponsored by [Hastings], are governed by this policy of nondiscrimination. [Has-
ting's] policy on nondiscrimination is to comply fully with applicable law.

"[Hastings] shall not discriminate unlawfully on the basis of race, color, religion,
national origin, ancestry, disability, age, sex or sexual orientation. This nondiscrimination policy covers admission, access and treatment in Hastings-sponsored programs and activities."

Hastings interprets the Nondiscrimination Policy, as it relates to the
RSO program, to mandate acceptance of all comers: School-approved
groups must "allow any student to participate, become a member, or

seek leadership positions in the organization, regardless of [her] status or beliefs." Other law schools have adopted similar all-comers policies.

From Hastings' adoption of its Nondiscrimination Policy in 1990 until the events stirring this litigation, "no student organization at Hastings ... ever sought an exemption from the Policy." In 2004, CLS became the first student group to do so. At the beginning of the academic year, the leaders of a predecessor Christian organization—which had been an RSO at Hastings for a decade—formed CLS by affiliating with the national Christian Legal Society (CLS-National). CLS-National, an association of Christian lawyers and law students, charters student chapters at law schools throughout the country. CLS chapters must adopt bylaws that require members and officers to sign a "Statement of Faith" and to conduct their lives in accord with prescribed principles. Among those tenets is the belief that sexual activity should not occur outside of marriage between a man and a woman; CLS thus interprets its bylaws to exclude from affiliation anyone who engages in "unrepentant homosexual conduct." CLS also excludes students who hold religious convictions different from those in the Statement of Faith.

On September 17, 2004, CLS submitted to Hastings an application for RSO status, accompanied by all required documents, including the set of bylaws mandated by CLS-National. Several days later, the Law School rejected the application; CLS's bylaws, Hastings explained, did not comply with the Nondiscrimination Policy because CLS barred students based on religion and sexual orientation.

CLS formally requested an exemption from the Nondiscrimination Policy, but Hastings declined to grant one. "[T]o be one of our student-recognized organizations," Hastings reiterated, "CLS must open its membership to all students irrespective of their religious beliefs or sexual orientation." If CLS instead chose to operate outside the RSO program, Hastings stated, the school "would be pleased to provide [CLS] the use of Hastings facilities for its meetings and activities." CLS would also have access to chalkboards and generally available campus bulletin boards to announce its events. In other words, Hastings would do nothing to suppress CLS's endeavors, but neither would it lend RSO-level support for them.

Refusing to alter its bylaws, CLS did not obtain RSO status. It did, however, operate independently during the 2004-2005 academic year. CLS held weekly Bible-study meetings and invited Hastings students to Good Friday and Easter Sunday church services. It also hosted a beach barbeque, Thanksgiving dinner, campus lecture on the Christian faith and the legal practice, several fellowship dinners, an end-of-year banquet, and other informal social activities. On October 22, 2004, CLS filed suit against various Hastings officers and administrators under 42 U.S.C. § 1983.

II

Before considering the merits of CLS's constitutional arguments, we must resolve a preliminary issue: CLS urges us to review the Nondiscrimination Policy as written—prohibiting discrimination on several enumerated bases, including religion and sexual orientation—and not as a requirement that all RSOs accept all comers. The written terms of the Nondiscrimination Policy, CLS contends, "targe[t] solely those groups whose beliefs are based on religion or that disapprove of a particular kind of sexual behavior," and leave other associations free to limit membership and leadership to individuals committed to the group's ideology. For example, "[a] political . . . group can insist that its leaders support its purposes and beliefs," CLS alleges, but "a religious group cannot."

CLS's assertion runs headlong into the stipulation of facts it jointly submitted with Hastings at the summary-judgment stage. In that filing, the parties specified: "Hastings requires that registered student organizations allow *any* student to participate, become a member, or seek leadership positions in the organization, regardless of [her] status or beliefs. Thus, for example, the Hastings Democratic Caucus cannot bar students holding Republican political beliefs from becoming members or seeking leadership positions in the organization."

"[Factual stipulations are] binding and conclusive . . . , and the facts stated are not subject to subsequent variation. So, the parties will not be permitted to deny the truth of the facts stated, . . . or to maintain a contention contrary to the agreed statement, . . . or to suggest, on appeal, that the facts were other than as stipulated or that any material fact was omitted." This Court has accordingly refused to consider a party's argument that contradicted a joint "stipulation [entered] at the outset of th[e] litigation." Time and again, the dissent races away from the facts to which CLS stipulated. But factual stipulations are "formal concessions . . . that have the effect of withdrawing a fact from issue and dispensing wholly with the need for proof of the fact. Thus, a judicial admission . . . is conclusive in the case."

In light of the joint stipulation, both the District Court and the Ninth Circuit trained their attention on the constitutionality of the all-comers requirement, as described in the parties' accord. We reject CLS's unseemly attempt to escape from the stipulation and shift its target to Hastings' policy as written. This opinion, therefore, considers only whether conditioning access to a student-organization forum on compliance with an all-comers policy violates the Constitution.

III

A

In support of the argument that Hastings' all-comers policy treads on its First Amendment rights to free speech and expressive association, CLS draws on two lines of decisions. First, in a progression of cases, this Court has employed forum analysis to determine when a governmental entity, in regulating property in its charge, may place limitations on speech. Recognizing a State's right "to preserve the property under its control for the use to which it is lawfully dedicated," the Court has permitted restrictions on access to a limited public forum, like the RSO program here, with this key caveat: Any access barrier must be reasonable and viewpoint neutral.

Second, as evidenced by another set of decisions, this Court has rigorously reviewed laws and regulations that constrain associational freedom. In the context of public accommodations, we have subjected restrictions on that freedom to close scrutiny; such restrictions are permitted only if they serve "compelling state interests" that are "unrelated to the suppression of ideas"—interests that cannot be advanced "through . . . significantly less restrictive [means]." "Freedom of association," we have recognized, "plainly presupposes a freedom not to associate." Insisting that an organization embrace unwelcome members, we have therefore concluded, "directly and immediately affects associational rights."

CLS would have us engage each line of cases independently, but its expressive-association and free-speech arguments merge: *Who* speaks on its behalf, CLS reasons, colors *what* concept is conveyed. It therefore makes little sense to treat CLS's speech and association claims as discrete. Instead, three observations lead us to conclude that our limited-public-forum precedents supply the appropriate framework for assessing both CLS's speech and association rights.

First, the same considerations that have led us to apply a less restrictive level of scrutiny to speech in limited public forums as compared to other environments, apply with equal force to expressive association occurring in limited public forums. As just noted, speech and expressive-association rights are closely linked.

Second, and closely related, the strict scrutiny we have applied in some settings to laws that burden expressive association would, in practical effect, invalidate a defining characteristic of limited public forums-the State may "reserv[e] [them] for certain groups."

Third, this case fits comfortably within the limited-public-forum category, for CLS, in seeking what is effectively a state subsidy, faces only indirect pressure to modify its membership policies; CLS may exclude any person for any reason if it forgoes the benefits of official recognition. The expressive-association precedents on which CLS relies, in contrast, involved regulations that *compelled* a group to include unwanted members, with no choice to opt out. In diverse contexts, our decisions have distinguished between policies that require action and those that withhold benefits.

In sum, we are persuaded that our limited-public-forum precedents adequately respect both CLS's speech and expressive-association rights, and fairly balance those rights against Hastings' interests as property owner and educational institution. We turn to the merits of the instant dispute, therefore, with the limited-public-forum decisions as our guide.

[B]

We first consider whether Hastings' policy is reasonable taking into account the RSO forum's function and "all the surrounding circumstances."

Our inquiry is shaped by the educational context in which it arises: "First Amendment rights," we have observed, "must be analyzed in light of the special characteristics of the school environment." This Court is the final arbiter of the question whether a public university has exceeded constitutional constraints, and we owe no deference to universities when we consider that question. Cognizant that judges lack the on-the-ground expertise and experience of school administrators, however, we have cautioned courts in various contexts to resist "substitut[ing] their own notions of sound educational policy for those of the school authorities which they review."

A college's commission—and its concomitant license to choose among pedagogical approaches—is not confined to the classroom, for extracurricular programs are, today, essential parts of the educational process. Schools, we have emphasized, enjoy "a significant measure of authority over the type of officially recognized activities in which their students participate." We therefore "approach our task with special caution," mindful that Hastings' decisions about the character of its student-group program are due decent respect.

With appropriate regard for school administrators' judgment, we review the justifications Hastings offers in defense of its all-comers requirement. First, the open-access policy "ensures that the leadership, educational, and social opportunities afforded by [RSOs] are available to all students." Just as "Hastings does not allow its professors to host classes open only to those students with a certain status or belief," so the Law School may decide, reasonably in our view, "that the . . . educational experience is best promoted when all participants in the forum must provide equal access to all students." RSOs, we count it significant, are eligible for financial assistance drawn from mandatory student-activity fees; the all-comers policy ensures that no Hastings student is forced to fund a group that would reject her as a member.

Second, the all-comers requirement helps Hastings police the written terms of its Nondiscrimination Policy without inquiring into an RSO's motivation for membership restrictions. To bring the RSO program within CLS's view of the Constitution's limits, CLS proposes that Hastings permit exclusion because of *belief* but forbid discrimination due to *status*. But that proposal would impose on Hastings a daunting labor. How should the Law School go about determining whether a student organization cloaked prohibited status exclusion in belief-based garb? If a hypothetical Male-Superiority Club barred a female student from running for its presidency, for example, how could the Law School tell whether the group rejected her bid because of her sex or because, by seeking to lead the club, she manifested a lack of belief in its fundamental philosophy?

Third, the Law School reasonably adheres to the view that an all-comers policy, to the extent it brings together individuals with diverse backgrounds and beliefs, "encourages tolerance, cooperation, and learning among students." And if the policy sometimes produces discord, Hastings can rationally rank among RSO-program goals development of conflict-resolution skills, toleration, and readiness to find common ground.

Fourth, Hastings' policy, which incorporates—in fact, subsumes—state-law proscriptions on discrimination, conveys the Law School's decision "to decline to subsidize with public monies and benefits conduct of which the people of California disapprove."

In sum, the several justifications Hastings asserts in support of its all-comers requirement are surely reasonable in light of the RSO forum's purposes.

The Law School's policy is all the more creditworthy in view of the "substantial alternative channels that remain open for [CLS-student] communication to take place." If restrictions on access to a limited public forum are viewpoint discriminatory, the ability of a group to exist outside the forum would not cure the constitutional shortcoming. But when access barriers are viewpoint neutral, our decisions have counted it significant that other available avenues for the group to exercise its First Amendment rights lessen the burden created by those barriers.

In this case, Hastings offered CLS access to school facilities to conduct meetings and the use of chalkboards and generally available bulletin boards to advertise events. Although CLS could not take advantage of RSO-specific methods of communication, the advent of electronic media and social-networking sites reduces the importance of those channels.

Private groups, from fraternities and sororities to social clubs and secret societies, commonly maintain a presence at universities without official school affiliation. Based on the record before us, CLS was similarly situated: It hosted a variety of activities the year after Hastings denied it recognition, and the number of students attending those meetings and events doubled. "The variety and type of alternative modes of access present here," in short, "compare favorably with those in other [limited public] forum cases where we have upheld restrictions on access."

CLS nevertheless deems Hastings' all-comers policy "frankly absurd." "There can be no diversity of viewpoints in a forum," it asserts, "if groups are not permitted to form around viewpoints." This catchphrase confuses CLS's preferred policy with constitutional limitation-the *advisability* of Hastings' policy does not control its *permissibility*. Instead, we have repeatedly stressed that a State's restriction on access to a limited public forum "need not be the most reasonable or the only reasonable limitation."

CLS also assails the reasonableness of the all-comers policy in light of the RSO forum's function by forecasting that the policy will facilitate hostile takeovers; if organizations must open their arms to all, CLS contends, saboteurs will infiltrate groups to subvert their mission and message. This supposition strikes us as more hypothetical than real. CLS points to no history or prospect of RSO-hijackings at Hastings. Students tend to self-sort and presumably will not endeavor en masse to join—let alone seek leadership positions in—groups pursuing missions wholly at odds with their personal beliefs. And if a rogue student intent on sabotaging an organization's objectives nevertheless attempted a takeover, the members of that group would not likely elect her as an officer.

RSOs, moreover, in harmony with the all-comers policy, may condition eligibility for membership and leadership on attendance, the payment of dues, or other neutral requirements designed to ensure that students join because of their commitment to a group's vitality, not its demise.

Hastings, furthermore, could reasonably expect more from its law students than the disruptive behavior CLS hypothesizes—and to build this expectation into its educational approach. A reasonable policy need not anticipate and preemptively close off every opportunity for avoidance or manipulation. If students begin to exploit an all-comers policy by hijacking organizations to distort or destroy their missions, Hastings presumably would revisit and revise its policy.

[C]

We next consider whether Hastings' all-comers policy is viewpoint neutral. Although this aspect of limited-public-forum analysis has been the constitutional sticking point in our prior decisions, as earlier recounted, we need not dwell on it here. It is, after all, hard to imagine a more viewpoint-neutral policy than one requiring *all* student groups to accept *all* comers.

Conceding that Hastings' all-comers policy is "nominally neutral," CLS attacks the regulation by pointing to its effect: The policy is vulnerable to constitutional assault, CLS contends, because "it systematically and predictably burdens most heavily those groups whose viewpoints are out of favor with the campus mainstream." Even if a regulation has a differential impact on groups wishing to enforce exclusionary membership policies, "[w]here the [State] does not target conduct on the basis of its expressive content, acts are not shielded from regulation merely because they express a discriminatory idea or philosophy."

Hastings' requirement that student groups accept all comers, we are satisfied, "is justified without reference to the content [or viewpoint] of the regulated speech." The Law School's policy aims at the *act* of rejecting would-be group members without reference to the reasons motivating that behavior: Hastings' "desire to redress th[e] perceived harms" of exclusionary membership policies "provides an adequate explanation for its [all-comers condition] over and above mere disagreement with [any student group's] beliefs or biases." CLS's conduct—not its Christian perspective—is, from Hastings' vantage point, what stands between the group and RSO status.

Finding Hastings' open-access condition on RSO status reasonable and viewpoint neutral, we reject CLS' free-speech and expressive-association claims.

IV

In its reply brief, CLS contends that "[t]he peculiarity, incoherence, and suspect history of the all-comers policy all point to pretext." Neither the District Court nor the Ninth Circuit addressed an argument that Hastings selectively enforces its all-comers policy, and this Court is not the proper forum to air the issue in the first instance. On remand, the Ninth Circuit may consider CLS's pretext argument if, and to the extent, it is preserved.

Justice KENNEDY, concurring.

To be effective, a limited forum often will exclude some speakers based on their affiliation (*e.g.,* student versus nonstudent) or based on the content of their speech, interests, and expertise (*e.g.,* art professor not chosen as speaker for conference on public transit). When the government does exclude from a limited forum, however, other content-based judgments may be impermissible. For instance, an otherwise qualified and relevant speaker may not be excluded because of hostility to his or her views or beliefs.

An objection might be that the all-comers policy, even if not so designed or intended, in fact makes it difficult for certain groups to express their views in a manner essential to their message. A group that can limit membership to those who agree in full with its aims and purposes may be more effective in delivering its message or furthering its expressive objectives; and the Court has recognized that this interest can be protected against governmental interference or regulation. By allowing like-minded students to form groups around shared identities, a school creates room for self-expression and personal development.

In the instant case, however, if the membership qualification were enforced, it would contradict a legitimate purpose for having created the limited forum in the first place. Many educational institutions, including respondent Hastings College of Law, have recognized that the process of learning occurs both formally in a classroom setting and informally outside of it. Students may be shaped as profoundly by their peers as by their teachers. Extracurricular activities, such as those in the Hastings "Registered Student Organization" program, facilitate interactions between students, enabling them to explore new points of view, to develop interests and talents, and to nurture a growing sense of self. The Hasting program is designed to allow all students to interact with their colleagues across a broad, seemingly unlimited range of ideas, views, and activities.

In addition to a circumstance, already noted, in which it could be demonstrated that a school has adopted or enforced its policy with the intent or purpose of discriminating or disadvantaging a group on account of its views, petitioner also would have a substantial case on the merits if it were shown that the all-comers policy was either designed or used to infiltrate the group or challenge its leadership in order to stifle its views. But that has not been shown to be so likely or self-evident as a matter of group dynamics in this setting that the Court can declare the school policy void without more facts; and if there were a showing that in a particular case the purpose or effect of the policy was to stifle speech or make it ineffective, that, too, would present a case different from the one before us.

Justice ALITO, with whom The CHIEF JUSTICE, Justice SCALIA, and Justice THOMAS join, dissenting.

The proudest boast of our free speech jurisprudence is that we protect the freedom to express "the thought that we hate." Today's decision rests on a very different principle: no freedom for expression that offends prevailing standards of political correctness in our country's institutions of higher learning.

The Hastings College of the Law, a state institution, permits student organizations to register with the law school and severely burdens speech by unregistered groups. Hastings currently has more than 60 registered groups and, in all its history, has denied registration to exactly one: the Christian Legal Society (CLS). CLS claims that Hastings refused to register the group because the law school administration disapproves of the group's viewpoint and thus violated the group's free speech rights.

The Court's treatment of this case is deeply disappointing. The Court does not address the constitutionality of the very different policy that Hastings invoked when it denied CLS's application for registration. Nor does the Court address the constitutionality of the policy that Hastings now purports to follow. And the Court ignores strong evidence that the accept-all-comers policy is not viewpoint neutral because it was announced as a pretext to justify viewpoint discrimination. Brushing aside inconvenient precedent, the Court arms public educational institutions with a handy weapon for suppressing the speech of unpopular groups-groups to which, as Hastings candidly puts it, these institutions "do not wish to . . . lend their name[s]."

I

The Court provides a misleading portrayal of this case. I begin by correcting the picture.

The Court bases all of its analysis on the proposition that the relevant Hastings' policy is the so-called accept-all-comers policy. This frees the Court from the difficult task of defending the constitutionality of either the policy that Hastings actually—and repeatedly—invoked when it denied registration, *i.e.,* the school's written Nondiscrimination Policy, or the policy that Hastings belatedly unveiled when it filed its brief in this Court. Overwhelming evidence, however, shows that Hastings denied CLS's application pursuant to the Nondiscrimination Policy and that the accept-all-comers policy was nowhere to be found until it was mentioned by a former dean in a deposition taken well after this case began.

During the 2004-2005 school year, Hastings had more than 60 registered groups, including political groups (*e.g.,* the Hastings Democratic Caucus and the Hastings Republicans), religious groups (*e.g.,* the Hastings Jewish Law Students Association and the Hastings Association of Muslim Law Students), groups that promote social causes (*e.g.,* both pro-choice and pro-life groups), groups organized around racial or ethnic identity (*e.g.,* the Black Law Students Association, the Korean American Law Society, La Raza Law Students Association, and the Middle Eastern Law Students Association), and groups that focus on gender or sexuality (*e.g.,* the Clara Foltz Feminist Association and Students Raising Consciousness at Hastings).

Not surprisingly many of these registered groups were and are dedicated to expressing a message. For example, Silenced Right, a pro-life group, taught that "all human life from the moment of conception until natural death is sacred and has inherent dignity," while Law Students for Choice aimed to "defend and expand reproductive rights.

Hastings claims that this accept-all-comers policy has existed since 1990 but points to no evidence that the policy was ever put in writing or brought to the attention of members of the law school community prior to the dean's deposition. Indeed, Hastings has adduced no evidence of the policy's existence before that date.

[T]he record is replete with evidence that, at least until Dean Kane unveiled the accept-all-comers policy in July 2005, Hastings routinely registered student groups with bylaws limiting membership and leadership positions to those who agreed with the groups' viewpoints. For example, the bylaws of the Hastings Democratic Caucus provided that "any full-time student at Hastings may become a member of HDC *so long as they do not exhibit a consistent disregard and lack of respect for the objective of the organization* as stated in Article 3, Section 1." The constitution of the Association of Trial Lawyers of America at Hastings provided that every member must "adhere to the objectives of the Student Chapter as well as the mission of ATLA." A student could become a member of the Vietnamese American Law Society so long as the student did not "exhibit a consistent disregard and lack of respect for the objective of the organization," which centers on a "celebrat[ion] [of] Vietnamese culture." Silenced Right limited voting membership to students who "are committed" to the group's "mission" of "spread[ing] the pro-life message." La Raza limited voting membership to "students of Raza background." Since Hastings requires any student group applying for registration to submit a copy of its bylaws, Hastings cannot claim that it was unaware of such provisions.

Like the majority of this Court, the Ninth Circuit relied on the following Joint Stipulation. I agree that the parties must be held to their Joint Stipulation, but the terms of the stipulation should be respected. What was admitted in the Joint Stipulation filed in December 2005 is that Hastings had an accept-all-comers policy. CLS did not stipulate that its application had been denied more than a year earlier pursuant to such a policy. On the contrary, the Joint Stipulation notes that the reason repeatedly given by Hasting at that time was that the CLS bylaws did not comply with *the Nondiscrimination Policy.* Indeed, the parties did not even stipulate that the accept-all-comers policy existed in the fall of 2004. In addition, Hastings itself is now attempting to walk away from this stipulation by disclosing that its real policy is an accept-some-comers policy.

The Court also distorts the record with respect to the effect on CLS of Hastings' decision to deny registration. The Court quotes a letter written by Hastings' general counsel in which she stated that Hastings "'would be pleased to provide [CLS] the use of Hastings facilities for its meetings and activities.'" Later in its opinion, the Court reiterates that "Hastings offered CLS access to school facilities to conduct meetings," but the majority does not mention that this offer was subject to important qualifications. As Hastings' attorney put it in the District Court, Hastings told CLS: "'Hastings allows community groups to some degree to use its facilities, sometimes on a pay basis, I understand, if they're available after priority is given to registered organizations'. We offered that."

Other statements in the majority opinion make it seem as if the denial of registration did not hurt CLS at all. The Court notes that CLS was able to hold Bible-study meetings and other events. And "[a]lthough CLS could not take advantage of RSO-specific methods of communication," the Court states, "the advent of electronic media and social-networking sites reduces the importance of those channels." At the beginning of the 2005 school year, the Hastings CLS group had seven members, so there can be no suggestion that the group flourished. And since one of CLS's principal claims is that it was subjected to discrimination based on its viewpoint, the majority's emphasis on CLS's ability to endure that discrimination-by using private facilities and means of communication-is quite amazing.

This Court does not customarily brush aside a claim of unlawful discrimination with the observation that the effects of the discrimination were really not so bad. We have never before taken the view that a little viewpoint discrimination is acceptable. Nor have we taken this approach in other discrimination cases.

C

Finally, I must comment on the majority's emphasis on funding. According to the majority, CLS is "seeking what is effectively a state subsidy," and the question presented in this case centers on the "use of school funds." In fact, funding plays a very small role in this case. Most of what CLS sought and was denied—such as permission to set up a table on the law school patio—would have been virtually cost free. If every such activity is regarded as a matter of funding, the First Amendment rights of students at public universities will be at the mercy of the administration. As CLS notes, "[t]o university students, the campus is their world. The right to meet on campus and use campus channels of communication is at least as important to university students as the right to gather on the town square and use local communication forums is to the citizen."

[II]

In this case, the forum consists of the RSO program. Once a public university opens a limited public forum, it "must respect the lawful boundaries it has itself set." The university "may not exclude speech where its distinction is not 'reasonable in light of the purpose served by the forum.'" And the university must maintain strict viewpoint neutrality.

This requirement of viewpoint neutrality extends to the expression of religious viewpoints. In an unbroken line of decisions analyzing private religious speech in limited public forums, we have made it perfectly clear that "[r]eligion is [a] viewpoint from which ideas are conveyed."

We have applied this analysis in cases in which student speech was restricted because of the speaker's religious viewpoint, and we have consistently concluded that such restrictions constitute viewpoint discrimination. We have also stressed that the rules applicable in a limited public forum are particularly important in the university setting, where "the State acts against a background of tradition of thought and experiment that is at the center of our intellectual and philosophic tradition."

Analyzed under this framework, Hastings' refusal to register CLS pursuant to its Nondiscrimination Policy plainly fails. As previously noted, when Hastings refused to register CLS, it claimed that the CLS bylaws impermissibly discriminated on the basis of religion and sexual orientation. As interpreted by Hastings and applied to CLS, both of these grounds constituted viewpoint discrimination.

As Hastings stated in its answer, the Nondiscrimination Policy "permit[ted] political, social, and cultural student organizations to select officers and members who are dedicated to a particular set of ideals or beliefs." But the policy singled out one category of expressive associations for disfavored treatment: groups formed to express a religious message. Only religious groups were required to admit students who did not share their views. An environmentalist group was not required to admit students who rejected global warming. An animal rights group was not obligated to accept students who supported the use of animals to test cosmetics. But CLS was required to admit avowed atheists. This was patent viewpoint discrimination. "By the very terms of the [Nondiscrimination Policy], the University . . . select [ed] for disfavored treatment those student [groups] with religious . . . viewpoints." It is no wonder that the Court makes no attempt to defend the constitutionality of the Nondiscrimination Policy.

The Hastings Nondiscrimination Policy, as interpreted by the law school, also discriminated on the basis of viewpoint regarding sexual morality. CLS has a particular viewpoint on this subject, namely, that sexual conduct outside marriage between a man and a woman is wrongful. Hastings would not allow CLS to express this viewpoint by limiting membership to persons willing to express a sincere agreement with CLS's views. By contrast, nothing in the Nondiscrimination Policy prohibited a group from expressing a contrary viewpoint by limiting membership to persons willing to endorse that group's beliefs. A Free Love Club could require members to affirm that they reject the traditional view of sexual morality to which CLS adheres. It is hard to see how this can be viewed as anything other than viewpoint discrimination.

The Court is also wrong in holding that the accept-all-comers policy is viewpoint neutral. The Court proclaims that it would be "hard to imagine a more viewpoint-neutral policy," but I would not be so quick to jump to this conclusion. Even if it is assumed that the policy is viewpoint neutral on its face, there is strong evidence in the record that the policy was announced as a pretext.

Here, CLS has made a strong showing that Hastings' sudden adoption and selective application of its accept-all-comers policy was a pretext for the law school's unlawful denial of CLS's registration application under the Nondiscrimination Policy.

Here, Hastings claims that it has had an accept-all-comers policy since 1990, but it has not produced a single written document memorializing that policy. Nor has it cited a single occasion prior to the dean's deposition when this putative policy was orally disclosed to either student groups interested in applying for registration or to the Office of Student Services, which was charged with reviewing the bylaws of applicant groups to ensure that they were in compliance with the law school's policies.

Since it appears that no one was told about the accept-all-comers policy before July 2005, it is not surprising that the policy was not enforced. The record is replete with evidence that Hastings made no effort to enforce the all-comers policy until after it was proclaimed by the former dean.

The Court—understandably—sidesteps this issue. The Court states that the lower courts did not address the "argument that Hastings selectively enforces its all-comer policy," that "this Court is not the proper forum to air the issue in the first instance," and that "[o]n remand, the Ninth Circuit may consider CLS's pretext argument if, and to the extent, it is preserved."

Because the Court affirms the entry of summary judgment in favor of respondents, it is not clear how CLS will be able to ask the Ninth Circuit on remand to review its claim of pretext. And the argument that we should not address this issue of pretext because the Ninth Circuit did not do so is hard to take, given that the Ninth Circuit barely addressed anything, disposing of this case in precisely two sentences.

[III]

One final aspect of the Court's decision warrants comment. In response to the argument that the accept-all-comers-policy would permit a small and unpopular group to be taken over by students who wish to silence its message, the Court states that the policy would permit a registered group to impose membership requirements "designed to ensure that students join because of their commitment to a group's vitality, not its demise."

With this concession, the Court tacitly recognizes that Hastings does not really have an accept-all-comers policy—it has an accept-some-dissident-comers policy—and the line between members who merely seek to change a group's message (who apparently must be admitted) and those who seek a group's "demise" (who may be kept out) is hopelessly vague.

Justice Kennedy takes a similarly mistaken tack. He contends that CLS "would have a substantial case on the merits if it were shown that the all-comers policy was . . . used to infiltrate the group or challenge its leadership in order to stifle its views," but he does not explain on what ground such a claim could succeed. The Court holds that the accept-all-comers policy is viewpoint neutral and reasonable in light of the purposes of the RSO forum. How could those characteristics be altered by a change in the membership of one of the forum's registered groups? No explanation is apparent.

In the end, the Court refuses to acknowledge the consequences of its holding. A true accept-all-comers policy permits small unpopular groups to be taken over by students who wish to change the views that the group expresses. Rules requiring that members attend meetings, pay dues, and behave politely, would not eliminate this threat.

The possibility of such takeovers, however, is by no means the most important effect of the Court's holding. There are religious groups that cannot in good conscience agree in their bylaws that they will admit persons who do not share their faith, and for these groups, the consequence of an accept-all-comers policy is marginalization. This is where the Court's decision leads.

* * *

I do not think it is an exaggeration to say that today's decision is a serious setback for freedom of expression in this country. Our First Amendment reflects a "profound national commitment to the principle that debate on public issues should be uninhibited, robust, and wide-open." Even if the United States is the only Nation that shares this commitment to the same extent, I would not change our law to conform to the international norm. I fear that the Court's decision marks a turn in that direction. Even those who find CLS's views objectionable should be concerned about the way the group has been treated-by Hastings, the Court of Appeals, and now this Court. I can only hope that this decision will turn out to be an aberration.